"WELCOME TO HELL"
Arbitrary Detention, Torture, and Extortion in Chechnya

Human Rights Watch
New York · Washington · London · Brussels

Copyright © October 2000 Human Rights Watch.
All Rights Reserved.
Printed in the United States of America.

ISBN: 1-56432-253-X
Library of Congress Catalog Card Number: 00-109421

Cover design by Rafael Jiménez

Addresses for Human Rights Watch
350 Fifth Avenue, 34th Floor, New York, NY 10118-3299
Tel: (212) 290-4700, Fax: (212) 736-1300, E-mail: hrwnyc@hrw.org

1630 Connecticut Avenue, N.W., Suite 500, Washington, DC 20009
Tel: (202) 612-4321, Fax: (202) 612-4333, E-mail: hrwdc@hrw.org

33 Islington High Street, N1 9LH London, UK
Tel: (171) 713-1995, Fax: (171) 713-1800, E-mail: hrwatchuk@gn.apc.org

15 Rue Van Campenhout, 1000 Brussels, Belgium
Tel: (2) 732-2009, Fax: (2) 732-0471, E-mail: hrwatcheu@skynet.be

Web Site Address: http://www.hrw.org

Listserv address: To subscribe to the list, send an e-mail message to majordomo@igc.apc.org with "subscribe hrw-news" in the body of the message (leave the subject line blank).

Human Rights Watch is dedicated to
protecting the human rights of people around the world.

We stand with victims and activists to prevent
discrimination, to uphold political freedom, to protect people from inhumane
conduct in wartime, and to bring offenders to justice.

We investigate and expose
human rights violations and hold abusers accountable.

We challenge governments and those who hold power to end abusive practices
and respect international human rights law.

We enlist the public and the international
community to support the cause of human rights for all.

HUMAN RIGHTS WATCH

Human Rights Watch conducts regular, systematic investigations of human rights abuses in some seventy countries around the world. Our reputation for timely, reliable disclosures has made us an essential source of information for those concerned with human rights. We address the human rights practices of governments of all political stripes, of all geopolitical alignments, and of all ethnic and religious persuasions. Human Rights Watch defends freedom of thought and expression, due process and equal protection of the law, and a vigorous civil society; we document and denounce murders, disappearances, torture, arbitrary imprisonment, discrimination, and other abuses of internationally recognized human rights. Our goal is to hold governments accountable if they transgress the rights of their people.

Human Rights Watch began in 1978 with the founding of its Europe and Central Asia division (then known as Helsinki Watch). Today, it also includes divisions covering Africa, the Americas, Asia, and the Middle East. In addition, it includes three thematic divisions on arms, children's rights, and women's rights. It maintains offices in New York, Washington, Los Angeles, London, Brussels, Moscow, Dushanbe, and Hong Kong. Human Rights Watch is an independent, nongovernmental organization, supported by contributions from private individuals and foundations worldwide. It accepts no government funds, directly or indirectly.

The staff includes Kenneth Roth, executive director; Michele Alexander, development director; Reed Brody, advocacy director; Carroll Bogert, communications director; Barbara Guglielmo, finance director; Jeri Laber special advisor; Lotte Leicht, Brussels office director; Patrick Minges, publications director; Susan Osnos, associate director; Maria Pignataro Nielsen, human resources director; Jemera Rone, counsel; Malcolm Smart, program director; Wilder Tayler, general counsel; and Joanna Weschler, United Nations representative. Jonathan Fanton is the chair of the board. Robert L. Bernstein is the founding chair.

The regional directors of Human Rights Watch are Peter Takirambudde, Africa; José Miguel Vivanco, Americas; Sidney Jones, Asia; Holly Cartner, Europe and Central Asia; and Hanny Megally, Middle East and North Africa. The thematic division directors are Joost R. Hiltermann, arms; Lois Whitman, children's; and Regan Ralph, women's.

The members of the board of directors are Jonathan Fanton, chair; Lisa Anderson, Robert L. Bernstein, David M. Brown, William Carmichael, Dorothy Cullman, Gina Despres, Irene Diamond, Adrian W. DeWind, Fiona Druckenmiller, Edith Everett, Michael E. Gellert, Vartan Gregorian, Alice H. Henkin, James F. Hoge, Stephen L. Kass, Marina Pinto Kaufman, Bruce Klatsky, Joanne Leedom-Ackerman, Josh Mailman, Yolanda T. Moses, Samuel K. Murumba, Andrew Nathan, Jane Olson, Peter Osnos, Kathleen Peratis, Bruce Rabb, Sigrid Rausing, Orville Schell, Sid Sheinberg, Gary G. Sick, Malcolm Smith, Domna Stanton, John J. Studzinski, and Maya Wiley. Robert L. Bernstein is the founding chair of Human Rights Watch.

ACKNOWLEDGMENTS

Human Rights Watch had a continuous research presence in Ingushetia from December 1999 to May 2000. Research for this report was conducted by Peter Bouckaert and Malcolm Hawkes, researchers; Alexander Petrov, deputy director of the Moscow office; and Johanna Bjorken and Max Marcus, consultants. The report was written by Johanna Bjorken and Peter Bouckaert. It was edited by Rachel Denber, deputy director of the Europe and Central Asia Division; Martina Vandenberg, researcher in the Women's Rights Division; Michael McClintock, deputy program director; and Dinah PoKempner, deputy general counsel. Special thanks also to Diederik Lohman, director of Human Rights Watch's Moscow office. Invaluable assistance was provided by Liuda Belova and Alexander Ovcharuk in the Moscow office; Alexander Frangos, coordinator for the Europe and Central Asia division; Rachel Bien and Maria Pulzetti, associates for the Europe and Central Asia division; and Patrick Minges, publications director. Human Rights Watch also wishes to thank its local staff in Ingushetia who worked tirelessly to help gather the information in this report.

We are deeply grateful to the Memorial Human Rights Center for their contribution to this report and their collegiality, in Moscow and in Ingushetia.

Most of all, we wish to express our gratitude to the many former detainees who agreed to share their stories with us, despite their fears of possible consequences. Many braved genuine danger to travel to Ingushetia to be interviewed by Human Rights Watch researchers. We hope that this report will contribute to ending the abuses in detention that they faced, and bringing those responsible for torture and other abuses to justice.

Human Rights Watch gratefully acknowledges the C.S. Mott Foundation, the Carnegie Corporation, the Henry M. Jackson Foundation, the Moriah Fund, and the John Merck Fund for their generous support.

A NOTE ON THE USE OF NAMES

Most of the persons interviewed for this report were Chechen detainees who had experienced severe beatings, torture, and other abuses in custody. They were detained and released in the first six months of 2000, but many continued to live in great fear of rearrest and further abuse in detention. Russian authorities in Chechnya use a computerized database to identify rebel suspects which could be used to track down witnesses identified by name. For these reasons, Human Rights Watch has changed the names of most of the witnesses who provided information for this report. Changed names are enclosed within quotation marks, clearly identified as such in footnotes (with the notation "not his/her real name" when first used) and are used consistently throughout the report.

GLOSSARY OF TERMS

Article 208: The part of the Russian Criminal Code that deals with the organization of or participation in illegal armed groups.

CPT: The Council of Europe Committee for the Prevention of Torture and Inhuman or Degrading Treatment or Punishment.

GAZ 53: A prisoner transport vehicle, with two compartments in the trailer that serve as holding cells. Also may be colloquially called *avtozak* or *voronok*.

IVS (*Izoliator vremenogo zaderzhania*): Temporary holding cell at a police station. Under the jurisdiction of the Interior Ministry.

Komendatura: Local police command post.

MChS (*Ministerstvo chrezvychainykh situatsiy*): The Russian Emergencies Situation Ministry, also sometimes called EMERCOM in English.

MVD (*Ministerstvo vnutrennykh del*): Interior Ministry.

OMON (*Otriad militsii osobogo naznachenia*): Special forces (riot police) under the jurisdiction of the Interior Ministry, not the Defense Ministry. The Russian government Unified Forces in Chechnya are composed of Defense Ministry and Interior Ministry forces.

Procuracy (*Prokuratura*): State agency responsible for both criminal investigation and prosecution, and human rights protection.

Propiska: Residency permit for one's official place of residence. The word "propiska" has been excluded from official use since 1995 when the government introduced *registratsiya* (registration). Registration may be permanent or temporary. In everyday use people still often say "propiska" instead of "registratsiya" without distinguishing between permanent and temporary.

SOBR (*Spetsialnye otriady bystrogo reagirovania*): Special rapid reaction forces.

SIZO (*Sledstvennyi izoliator*): Pretrial detention center. Under the jurisdiction of the Ministry of Justice.

Chechnya

Welcome to hell. You're lost now. You will die a slow and painful death. We will teach you to respect Russian officers.
> Reported comments of Russian guards to detainee at Chernokozovo.

They used the iron part of their sticks to beat me on the bottoms of my feet. They put a cloth in my mouth so I couldn't scream, and they handcuffed me. They made me lay down on my stomach with my head under the table. They took off my boots and socks, and beat my soles, especially on the heels. Then they made me stand against the wall with my hands up, lifted my shirt and beat me on the kidneys with the sticks.
> Former detainee describing torture at Chernokozovo.

I heard the soldiers say while they were kicking me on the floor, 'Let's fuck him.' Then they said 'we won't dirty ourselves.' ... I was taken from the cell, and by the time I got to the questioning room, I was already only half-conscious. I was taken from this room to another where they said they would fuck me. It was February 7, late at night. I was lying on the floor, two guards held my legs while another kicked me in the testicles. I lost consciousness and would come around, I lost consciousness four times. They hit me around the head, there was blood. They would beat me unconscious and wait until I came round: 'He's woken up,' and they would come in and beat me [again].
> Former Chernokozovo inmate.

TABLE OF CONTENTS

SUMMARY 1
   Mass Arrests and Arbitrary Detention 2
   Torture and Other Abuse at Chernokozovo 3
   Abuses and Torture at Other Places of Detention 4
   The Business of Release: Extortion and "Amnesties" 5
   Incommunicado Detention and "Disappearances" 5

INTRODUCTION 6

LEGAL STANDARDS 9
   International Standards 12
   Domestic Standards 12
   The Duty to Investigate 13

THE PROCESS OF DETENTION 17
   Arrests at Checkpoints and Border Crossings 18
   Arrests in the context of "mop-up" operations 20
   Arrests during targeted sweeps of communities 23

THE CHERNOKOZOVO DETENTION CENTER 26
   Introduction 26
   Beatings and other torture at Chernokozovo 29
      The Human Corridor 29
      Torture in the Context of Interrogations 32
      Night Beatings: "They were out of control" 40
         Humiliating "games" 42
         Physical Exhaustion 43
      Rape 45
   The "Cleanup" 48
      The Russian Commission Visit 48
      International Outrage and Russian Denial 50

ABUSES AND TORTURE IN OTHER PLACES OF DETENTION 55
   Stavropol territory 56
   Military bases 58
      Mozdok 58
      Khankala 60
      Other Military Encampments 64
   Other Ad-hoc Detention Centers 67

    Tolstoy Yurt 67
    The Internat in Urus-Martan 69
    Local Police Stations or Command Posts, and Abuse in Transit 73

THE BUSINESS OF RELEASE: EXTORTION, "AMNESTIES,"
    AND THE THREAT OF RE-ARREST 77
    Extortion 77
    Rearrest and the Threat of Rearrest 81

OTHER VIOLATIONS OF THE RIGHTS OF INDIVIDUALS DEPRIVED OF
    THEIR LIBERTY 83
    Prolonged Incommunicado Detention and "Disappearances" 83
    Denial of access to legal counsel 85

RECOMMENDATIONS 89
    To the Government of the Russian Federation 89
    To the Special Representative for Human Rights in Chechnya Vladimir
        Kalamanov 91
    To the International Community 92
        United Nations 93
        To the Council of Europe 93
        To the Organization for Security and Cooperation in Europe 95
        To the International Monetary Fund, the World Bank, the European
            Bank for Reconstruction and Development and Bilateral Donors 96
        To the European Union and the United States 96

APPENDIX 1: KNOWN PLACES OF DETENTION IN CHECHNYA 98

SUMMARY

Chechen detainees who arrived at the Russian Chernokozovo "filtration" camp in January 2000 received an ominous welcome. "Welcome to hell," the prison guards would say, and then force them to walk through a human corridor of baton-wielding guards. This was only the beginning of a ghastly cycle of abuse for most detainees in early 2000, who suffered systematic beatings, rape, and other forms of torture. Most were released only after their families managed to pay large sums to Russian officials bent on extortion.

Those forced to run the gauntlet were among the thousands of Chechens detained by Russian forces on suspicion of collaboration with rebel fighters. Since September 1999, Russia has waged a military campaign to reestablish control over Chechnya that has cost thousands of civilian lives, displaced hundreds of thousands of people, and caused massive destruction to civilian infrastructure. Civilians bore the brunt of Russian forces' indiscriminate and disproportionate bombardments, of summary executions, and other violations of the rules of internal armed conflict.

Although the military offensive tapered off by April 2000, tens of thousands of displaced Chechens fear returning home lest they or their husbands, sons, fathers, or brothers be arrested or killed by Russian forces. Thousands more in Chechnya do not dare leave their communities, even to seek medical treatment. There is a lot to fear: by the end of May 2000, the Ministry of Interior claimed that more than ten thousand people had been arrested in Chechnya since the beginning of 2000, of whom 478 were on the "wanted list," and more than a thousand of whom were "[Chechen] rebels and their accomplices."[1] Arrests continued throughout Chechnya as this report went to press. Most of the detained we1re taken to detention centers set up throughout Chechnya and elsewhere in the North Caucasus, where they were subjected to severe abuses.

This report documents arbitrary arrests and the abuses that occur in detention in Chechnya, focusing on Chernokozovo and six other detention facilities identified in the region: in Tolstoy-Yurt, Khankala, and Urus-Martan, all in Chechnya; in Pyatigorsk and Stavropol, in Stavropol province, and in Mozdok, North Ossetia. It is based on the work of Human Rights Watch researchers who identified and interviewed dozens of former detainees over a four-month period from February to May 2000, carefully cross-checking and corroborating individual accounts with the information gathered from other interviews.

The torture and other abuse documented in this report are serious violations of Russia's obligations under the Geneva Conventions of 1949, and of Protocol II to

---

[1] "RIA reports results of successful crime fighting in Chechnya in 2000," RIA News Agency/BBC Monitoring, May 28, 2000.

the convention which elaborates the rules for internal armed conflict, and under the instruments of international human rights law to which Russia is also party.

Arbitrary arrest and torture in detention centers are not a new phenomenon in Chechnya. During the 1994-1996 Chechen war, Russian forces also rounded up thousands of Chechen civilians and took them for interrogation to detention centers in Mozdok, Grozny, Pyatigorsk, and Stavropol. Detainees were abused and tortured in these camps during the first war, and frequently were exchanged for captured Russian soldiers or cash. Many detainees never came home, "disappearing" forever following their detention by Russian forces.

Mass Arrests and Arbitrary Detention

As soon as armed conflict resumed in Chechnya in September 1999, Russian authorities began arresting men and women at checkpoints, during sweeps that followed military hostilities, and in targeted sweeps of communities. Although Russia has not declared a state of emergency in Chechnya, due process rights are routinely ignored in the arrest process. Detained persons are frequently held incommunicado, and many remain in unacknowledged detention, "disappeared" months after their arrest. The grounds for detention are often wholly arbitrary: men and women are detained simply because they are found in locations that are not their official, permanent address, because their documents are incomplete, because they share a surname with a Chechen commander, because they are perceived to have relatives who are fighters, or because they "look" like fighters.

Chechens are so commonly detained at checkpoints within Chechnya and along Chechnya's borders with other parts of Russia that many have gone to great lengths to avoid travel altogether, even when they need to flee active fighting. Checkpoint officials are often abusive towards fleeing civilians, particularly towards young males. Men were regularly beaten during the detention process, and frequently subjected to taunts and threats. On occasion, women have been raped at checkpoints after being detained: Human Rights documented the rape of two young women at the main Kavkaz border crossing in late January 2000.

Russian forces commonly rounded up and detained groups of Chechen men in "mop-ups," or operations to flush out or detain rebels and their collaborators, following the takeover of Chechen communities. Russian forces also carry out arrest sweeps and house-to-house searches after guerrilla ambushes or other attacks. In some cases, the male population of a village was rounded up, taken to an empty field, and subjected to beatings while Russian officials looked for suspected rebels. Those rounded up in mop-up or sweep operations are treated especially harshly: Russian forces beat them mercilessly, sometimes to death, and have summarily executed others. In one case, Akhmed Doshaev was summarily executed by Russian soldiers after being arrested in Shaami-Yurt on February 5, 2000.

Torture and Other Abuse at Chernokozovo

During January and early February 2000, when the war was in its most intense phase, the remand prison at Chernokozovo, located some sixty kilometers northwest of Grozny, was the principal destination for detainees in Chechnya. Detainees arriving at Chernokozovo were met by two lines of baton-wielding guards forming a human gauntlet, and received a punishing beating before entering the facility. At least one detainee, Aindi Kovtorashvilli, died at the facility on January 11, 2000, when an earlier head wound was aggravated during the intake beating.

Detainees at Chernokozovo were beaten both during interrogation and during nighttime sessions when guards utterly ran amok. During interrogation, detainees were forced to crawl on the ground and were beaten so severely that some sustained broken ribs and injuries to their kidneys, liver, testicles, and feet.[2] Some were also tortured with electric shocks.

At night, guards were given free rein for wanton abuse and humiliation. Often drunk and playing loud music, guards would subject detainees to beatings and humiliating games. Some of the most severe beatings took place at night: detainees report being beaten unconscious, only to be revived and beaten again. Detainees were forced to crawl across rooms with guards on their backs, and were beaten if they performed too slowly. In their cells, detainees were ordered to stand with their hands raised for entire days, and guards used teargas if their orders were disobeyed. Convincing evidence exists that men and women were raped and sexually assaulted with police batons at Chernokozovo.

In mid-February, amid mounting international attention to human rights abuses in Chechnya and calls for visits by international delegations, Russian authorities ordered a clean-up of the Chernokozovo facility. A visit in early February 2000 by Russian military officials found serious evidence of abuse, even though many abused inmates were removed from the facility prior to the visit and others were warned not to complain. By the time international monitors and journalists visited the facility in late February 2000, conditions had improved and most of the evidence of abuse had been removed. Russian officials, including presidential spokesman Sergei Yastrzhembsky and special presidential representative for human rights Vladimir Kalamanov, issued blanket denials about abuses at Chernokozovo. To date, there has been no formal investigation into the abuse at Chernokozovo.

---

[2]Beating of the feet, commonly referred to as *falanga*, *falaka*, or *basinado*, is a widely recognized form of torture which can have severe consequences, including muscle necrosis, vascular obstruction, and chronic disability and pain. See Action Against Torture Survivors et al., *Manual on the Effective Investigation and Documentation of Torture and Other Cruel, Inhuman or Degrading Treatment or Punishment* ("The Istanbul Protocol"), August 1999, for a detailed medical description of the effects of *falanga* torture.

Abuses and Torture at Other Places of Detention

Improvements in conditions at Chernokozovo by mid-February did not bring relief for the increasing number of detainees who were taken to other detention places. Detainees continued to suffer abuses at checkpoints, police stations, military bases, and prisons within and beyond Chechnya.

At remand prisons in Stavropol and Pyatigorsk, both located in the Stavropol territory, detainees were also met with a gauntlet of soldiers who beat them with batons, and suffered continuing severe beatings while at the detention facilities. At Mozdok military base, detainees were sodomized with batons, forced to walk between ranks of guards while being beaten and kicked, and beaten in their testicles. A doctor in Ingushetia reported receiving a patient who had been detained at Mozdok who had severely swollen genitals and appeared to have been raped, as he suffered from internal injuries to the colon.

At the large Khankala military base outside Grozny detainees were often kept in overcrowded prisoner transport vehicles, even during the bitter cold of winter. A nineteen-year-old woman who was believed to be mentally retarded was raped at Khankala for three days by numerous soldiers at the end of January 2000. Men were severely beaten there, including during interrogations, and at least one was tortured with a soldering iron. In April, two badly disfigured corpses were recovered from Khankala, and it is likely that the two men were tortured and executed at the facility.

Abuses also took place at military encampments around Chechnya. Zhebir Turpalkhanov was detained in April 2000 at an encampment near Tsotsin-Yurt and severely beaten for five days during his detention; he died just hours after his release.

Detainees were also kept at a disused oil refinery near Tolstoy-Yurt, where abuses included threats of summary execution and beatings—some so severe that they led to broken ribs. At a former boarding school in Urus-Martan, one of three detention facilities in the town, detainees were forced to walk through a gauntlet of baton-wielding guards and were subjected to frequent beatings; one inmate was reportedly raped as recently as April 2000.

Upon arrest, detainees were often first taken to police stations before being transported to detention centers. Many detainees from Grozny went first to the Znamenskoye police station, where they were beaten and kicked upon arrival and in their cells. When detainees were transported from Znamenskoye, they were sometimes stacked on top of each other like logs, causing detainees at the bottom of the pile to lose consciousness. Human Rights Watch has also documented similar physical abuse and beatings at other police posts.

The Business of Release: Extortion and "Amnesties"
The majority of former detainees interviewed by Human Rights Watch reported that they were only released after their families had paid substantial bribes to their Russian captors and predatory intermediaries, ranging from 2,000 rubles to U.S. $5,000. In fact, bribes were demanded for release so often that in many cases, detention itself appears to have been motivated by the promise of financial gain, rather than by the need to identify rebel elements. One man detained by OMON troops near Komsomolskoye in late January 2000 was never turned over to investigative authorities; instead, his captors immediately opened negotiations with the family for his release.

The guilt or innocence of the detainee seem to have little impact on the extortion process, except on the amount of money involved: innocence alone is not enough to secure release, and even confirmed Chechen fighters can be bought out for the appropriate amount. In one documented case, the head of a village administration secured the release of a captured fighter for U.S. $5,000. In most cases, relatives are approached by middlemen preying on their desperation to extort large sums for the release of the detained relative.

Russian officials often refuse to return important identity documents to detainees upon release, or release detainees with documents identifying them as "amnestied fighters," even when involvement in armed activity was never established. This curtails the freedom of movement of the released detainee, as they are unable to travel through checkpoints for fear of rearrest, harassment, or other abuse. Detainees released without documents become virtual prisoners in their home districts.

Incommunicado Detention and "Disappearances"
Russian authorities withhold information about whom they have in custody, and do not allow detainees to communicate with their families, even when detained for months. As a result, relatives travel to detention facilities, desperately trying to establish the whereabouts of their loved ones. Many maintain a steady vigil outside the detention centers where they believe their relatives are kept, and constantly exchange information among themselves about other known detention facilities and lists of names of known detainees, smuggled out by those who are released.

INTRODUCTION

The current military campaign in Chechnya started in September 1999. It was sparked that month by a Chechen armed incursion into the neighboring republic of Dagestan and several bombings in Russia, which the Russian government quickly blamed on Chechen forces. Russia's military campaign in Chechnya has been characterized by widespread human rights abuses and violations of the laws of war, including mass killings of civilians, indiscriminate bombing and shelling, and widespread pillage.[3]

After advancing quickly through northern Chechnya, taking many towns without a fight—including Chechnya's second-largest city, Gudermes—Russian forces began focusing their offensive on the Chechen capital, Grozny. In early January, Chechen fighters in Grozny caught Russian forces by surprise when they broke out of the capital and temporarily took control of several towns surrounding it, including Alkhan-Kala, Gudermes, Argun and Shali.[4] Gen. Viktor Kazantsev, who at the time was Russia's commander of the United Group of Forces in Chechnya, quickly blamed the setbacks on the "tenderheartedness" of Russian troops and their "groundless trust" in Chechen civilians.[5] General Kazantsev ordered Chechnya's internal borders closed to all men between the ages of ten and sixty, and stated that all men between those ages would be taken to a "filtration

---

[3] For more information on abuses in the war in Chechnya, see the Human Rights Watch website, www.hrw.org. In addition to many press releases documenting abuses, Human Rights Watch has issued three reports since the resumption of hostilities in Chechnya: "February 5: A Day of Slaughter in Novye Aldi," a *Human Rights Watch Short Report*, vol. 12, no. 9(D), June 2000; "No Happiness Remains: Civilian Killings, Pillage, and Rape in Alkhan-Yurt," a *Human Rights Watch Short Report*, vol. 12, no. 5(D), April 2000; and "Civilian Killings in the Staropromyslovski District of Grozny," a *Human Rights Watch Short Report*, vol. 12, no. 2(D), February 2000. These reports are available in English and Russian. Other human rights organizations have also extensively documented abuses in the conflict in Chechnya; see for example, Amnesty International, *Russian Federation: Chechnya. For the Motherland*, December 1999 EUR 46/46/99; the respected Russian human rights organization Memorial, (on the internet at www.memorial.ru), and Medicins du Monde.

[4] See Michael Gordon, "Troops Try to Regain Footing in Chechnya After Rebel Strikes," *New York Times*, January 11, 2000.

[5] Daniel Williams, "Russians to Detain Males in Chechnya: General Criticizes Troops for Trusting Civilians," *Washington Post*, January 12, 2000.

camp," Chernokozovo, to be investigated for rebel affiliation.[6] Almost immediately, Russian forces in Chechnya began detaining men in this age range and sending them to a prison facility in Chernokozovo, in northern Chechnya.

In February 2000, Chechen rebel fighters abandoned Grozny and set out for the mountains of southern Chechnya to continue their fighting. Russian forces responded with further widespread arrests of Chechen males, most of them civilians without rebel affiliation. In several cases, more than one hundred male civilians were arrested in a single incident. About the same time, the first detainees from the Chernokozovo detention facilities began to be released, and spoke out about appalling abuses there. The international community reacted with outrage to the allegations and pressured Russia to end the abuses at Chernokozovo and to open the facility to outside scrutiny.

In response to intense criticism, the Russian government made some improvements to the Chernokozovo facility, and then allowed limited access to it for international agencies. Prior to visits by foreign journalists and Council of Europe delegations, detainees were transferred temporarily to conceal the overcrowded conditions as well as the abuse they had suffered. The guards warned inmates not to speak candidly with visitors, and punished those who did.

As spring arrived, Chechen fighters attempted to disrupt Russian forces efforts to consolidate control over the lowlands by launching periodic ambushes and other attacks on Russian targets. Russian forces—in most cases riot police—frequently responded with round-ups of Chechens, ostensibly those suspected of affiliation with the fighters. As arrests continued, the Russian authorities decentralized their operation, holding suspects at facilities closer to the place of arrest, only later to transfer some to the spruced-up Chernokozovo and different, lesser-known detention facilities.

This report deals exclusively with abuses committed by Russian forces against those deprived of their liberty. Russian authorities frequently deflect criticism of the human rights violations committed in Chechnya by referring to the appalling

---

[6]Daniel Williams, General Kazantsev also stated that "only children up to the age of ten, men over sixty, and women, will henceforth be regarded as refugees." Human Rights Watch press release, "Russia Closes Borders to Chechen Males: Blanket Ban Traps Men in War Zone," January 12, 2000. In the 1994-1995 conflict in Chechnya "filtration camps" were detention centers run by Russian forces ostensibly to weed out Chechen rebels and to gain information about rebel activities. See Human Rights Watch/Helsinki, "Russia/Chechnya: A Legacy of Abuse," *A Human Rights Watch Report*, vol. 9, no. 2(D), January, 1997. Russian forces were notorious for subjecting "filtration camp" inmates to repeated beatings and other torture. See Memorial Human Rights Center, *Conditions in Detention in Chechen Republic Conflict Zone, Treatment of Detainees* (Moscow, 1995).

abuses committed by the Chechen side, which in this and previous conflicts have included summary execution, including by beheading, kidnaping, rape, torture and ill-treatment, and general violation of civilian immunities. Other Human Rights Watch reports and press releases have documented abuses by Chechen forces in the current conflict. However, violations committed by one side can never be used to justify violations committed by the other.

LEGAL STANDARDS

International Standards

Torture, physical abuse, arbitrary arrest, "disappearances," summary executions, rape, and the failure to accord procedural rights to persons in detention and at trial violate international human rights norms binding upon Russia, in particular those codified in the International Covenant on Civil and Political Rights (ICCPR) and the Convention against Torture and Other Cruel, Inhuman or Degrading Treatment or Punishment (Convention Against Torture). Russia is also a party to the European Convention on Human Rights (ECHR), and subject to the jurisdiction of the European Court of Human Rights, the body which enforces the ECHR.[7]

The provisions of international humanitarian law, also known as the laws of war, which came into play with the renewed outbreak of armed conflict in Chechnya, bar much of the same conduct, an essential difference being the combatant's "privilege" to take part in hostilities, including acting to kill or harm opposing combatants. Russia is party to the four Geneva Conventions of 1949 and their two Protocols.[8] The fighting in Chechnya unquestionably has been intense enough to qualify as "armed conflict," making applicable the laws of war. The armed conflict is of a "non-international" character and thus governed by Article 3 common to the four Geneva Conventions of 1949 and Protocol II.[9]

The most grievous affront to basic international human rights and humanitarian norms documented in this report is the violation of the right to life. Article 6(1) of

---

[7] Derogation from certain human rights norms, such as procedural rights, are permitted in officially declared public emergencies threatening the life of the nation. However, Russia has not declared a state of emergency in Chechnya under either the procedures of the ICCPR or the ECHR.

[8] The protections that humanitarian law affords non-combatants, by design applicable in time of war, are not subject to derogation.

[9] Article 1 of Protocol II states it applies, inter alia, to those armed conflicts between a party to the treaty and "dissident armed forces or other organized armed groups which, under responsible command, exercise such control over a part of its territory as to enable them to carry out sustained and concerted military operations and to implement this Protocol." Chechen separatist forces fit this description. Indeed, in May 2000, Chechen President Aslan Maskhadov wrote to the Swiss Federal Council, indicating that the separatist Chechen republic wanted to accede to the four Geneva Conventions and their two additional protocols. "Chechen Rebels bid for Geneva Conventions status," *Associated Press*, May 6, 2000. As Chechnya is not recognized as an independent state, it is not able to become a party to these treaties, although rebel forces, as inhabitants of states parties, are deemed to be bound by these humanitarian norms as well.

the ICCPR provides "No one shall be arbitrarily deprived of his life," and article 2 of the ECHR similarly bars intentional killing except in very narrow circumstances. With respect to non-combatants, Common Article 3 prohibits "at any time and in any place whatsoever ... violence to life and person, in particular murder of all kinds," and "the passing of sentences and carrying out of executions without previous judgement pronounced by a regularly constituted court." Protocol II articulates the same prohibitions in similar language at articles 2 and 6. These standards would all apply without possibility of derogation to forbid the extrajudicial execution of detainees.

Few elements of international human rights law are as unequivocal as the ban on torture. The prohibition is embodied in the United Nations Universal Declaration on Human Rights, which states in Article 5: "No one shall be subjected to torture or to cruel, inhuman or degrading treatment or punishment." That right is reaffirmed verbatim in article 7 of the ICCPR and article 3 of the ECHR. The Convention against Torture, article 1(1), defines torture as:

> any act by which severe pain or suffering, whether physical or mental, is intentionally inflicted on a person for such purposes as obtaining from him or a third person information or a confession, punishing him for an act he or a third person has committed, or intimidating or coercing him or a third person, or for any reason based on discrimination of any kind, when such pain or suffering is inflicted by or at the instigation of or with the consent or acquiescence of a public official or other person acting in an official capacity. It does not include pain or suffering arising only from, inherent in or incidental to lawful sanctions.

Article 15 of the Convention against Torture requires states parties to ensure that statements obtained through torture not be used as evidence in any proceedings, except against a person accused of torture as evidence that the statement was made. Common Article 3 of the Geneva Conventions and Protocol II likewise prohibit violence to the physical and mental well-being of the person, including mutilation, cruel treatment and torture as well as "outrages upon personal dignity, in particular humiliating and degrading treatment."[10]

Rape and other forms of sexual violence fall within the prohibition of "cruel, inhuman or degrading treatment" prohibited under the human rights treaties, and

---

[10] Common Article 3(1) to the Geneva Conventions of 1949 and Protocol II, art. 4(2).

indeed, may often rise to the level of torture.[11] These acts are also explicitly and implicitly condemned by international humanitarian law.[12]

Even where the act of sexual violence was not technically rape, or did not cause severe physical pain or suffering, it still may rise to the level of torture or other cruel, inhuman or degrading treatment on account of the psychological suffering inflicted. In interviews, some women detainees spoke of being forced to strip naked during interrogations. The *Akayesu Judgment* of the International Criminal Tribunal for Rwanda (ICTR) established a broad definition of sexual violence: "Sexual violence is not limited to physical invasion of the human body and may include acts which do not involve penetration or even physical contact," including forced nudity.[13]

Arbitrary arrest or detention is prohibited by Article 9 of the ICCPR. To comply with Article 9, the state must specify in its legislation the grounds on which individuals may be deprived of their liberty and the procedures to be used in enforcing arrests and detentions. Only acts conducted in accordance with such rules are considered lawful, thus restricting the discretion of individual arresting officers. Moreover, the prohibition on arbitrariness means that the deprivation of liberty, even if provided for by law, must still be proportional to the reasons for arrest, as well as predictable. Article 9 also specifically requires that detainees be immediately informed of the reasons for their arrest and promptly be told of any charges against them, and that they be brought promptly before a judge empowered to rule upon the lawfulness of the detention. Article 5 of the ECHR contains similar guarantees.

The manner in which Russian authorities have rounded up and detained civilians in Chechnya must be considered arbitrary. Grounds cited for detention often were alleged irregularities with identification documents. Under Russian law, police officers are allowed to detain an individual for up to three hours to establish his or her identity, but only if the officer has sufficient grounds to suspect that the

---

[11] See "Report of the U.N. Special Rapporteur on Torture," Mr. Nigel S. Rodley, submitted pursuant to the Commission on Human Rights Resolution 1992/32.E/CN.4/1995/34, Paragraph 19, January 12, 1995. See also *Aydin v. Turkey*, VI Eur. Ct. H.R. (1977).

[12] In internal armed conflicts, such as the Chechen conflict, common Article 3 of the Geneva Conventions prohibits "outrages upon personal dignity, in particular humiliating and degrading treatment," while Protocol II is even more explicit, expressly prohibiting "outrages upon personal dignity, in particular humiliating and degrading treatment, rape, enforced prostitution and any form of indecent assault."

[13] *Akayesu Judgment*, ICTR-96-4-T, Trial Chamber 1, 2 September 1998, paragraph 688.

individual has committed an administrative or criminal offense.[14] But as documented in this report, civilians were detained for weeks or even months for alleged passport irregularities, and detaining authorities rarely stated other grounds to justify the arrest. When civilians were detained for being in locations that were not their legal permanent address, this not only constituted arbitrary arrest, but also violated their rights to freedom of movement. Often, however, no grounds at all for arrests were given.

Domestic Standards

Russia has not declared a state of emergency in Chechnya, and thus Russia's domestic legal obligations, including the constitutional rights of citizens, remain in full force in the war-torn republic. Russia remains obligated to fully adhere to these rights without derogation.

Torture and physical abuse are punishable crimes under the Russian legal code, although the legal definition of torture in Russian law does not cover the full scope of the definition contained in the Convention against Torture. Article 21(2) of the Russian constitution states in relevant part that "[no] one may be subjected to torture, violence or other treatment or punishment that is cruel or degrading to the human dignity."[15] Article 111 of Russia's criminal code sets penalties of two to fifteen years of imprisonment for the infliction of serious bodily injury, but does not specifically address persons acting in an official capacity.[16] Article 117 of the criminal code, which also does not address persons acting in an official capacity, addresses ill-treatment:

> Infliction of physical or psychological suffering by administering systematic beatings or other violent means, if this did not have the consequences indicated in article 111 [severe damage to health] and 112 [damage to health of average seriousness] of this law is punishable by deprivation of freedom for up to three years.

The Russian criminal procedure code bans the coercion of "a defendant or other participant in a case to give testimony by means of violence, threats or other unlawful means,"[17] and since March 1999 the law on police also forbids the use of

---

[14] Law of the Russian Federation on the Police, article 11(2).
[15] Constitution of the Russian Federation (1993), Article 21(2).
[16] Criminal Code of the Russian Federation (entered into force 1997), Article 111.
[17] Criminal Procedure Code of the RSFSR (1962, as amended), Article 20(3).

torture and ill-treatment.[18] Torture committed by an official is considered an aggravated circumstance of the crime of coercion to give testimony, defined in article 302 of the criminal code:

> 1. Coercion of a suspect, defendant, victim [of crime] or witness into giving testimony or coercion of an expert into giving a conclusion by means of threats, blackmail or other unlawful means by an investigator or person carrying out the inquiry is punishable by deprivation of freedom for a period of up to three years.
>
> 2. The same action, together with the application of violence, degrading treatment or torture is punishable by deprivation of freedom for a period of two to eight years.

Summary or arbitrary executions are acts of murder, and are punishable as such under the Russian criminal code. Similarly, rape is a punishable offense under the Russian criminal code.

The Duty to Investigate

Under international law, Russia has a duty to investigate allegations of torture, rape, summary execution and other serious violations of human rights and international humanitarian law standards. The perpetrators of such abuses should be punished, and victims should be provided with compensation.

Article 12 of the Convention against Torture obliges states parties to initiate a prompt and impartial investigation of torture complaints whenever circumstances give "reasonable ground to believe that an act of torture has been committed." Article 13 of the ECHR requires states to establish "an effective remedy before a national authority" for anyone whose rights and freedoms
as set out in the convention have been violated. In addition, the European Court of Human Rights has ruled that article 1 of the ECHR, in conjunction with article 3, requires an effective investigation of torture complaints whenever the applicant has

---

[18] Article 5 of the Law of RSFSR on Police, as amended on March 31, 1999, published in *Rossiiskaia gazeta*, April 8, 1999, p. 5. It states: "Police may not use torture, violence or other forms of cruel or degrading treatment."

an "arguable claim."[19] For example, in the case of *Assenov and others v. Bulgaria* it stated:

> The Court considers that, in these circumstances, where an individual raises an arguable claim that he has been seriously ill-treated by the police or other agents of the State unlawfully and in breach of Article 3, that provision, read in conjunction with the State's general duty under Article 1 of the Convention to "secure to everyone within their jurisdiction the rights and freedoms in [the] Convention," requires by implication that there should be an effective official investigation [of alleged violations of the rights set forth in the Convention.] This obligation...should be capable of leading to the identification and punishment of those responsible.[20]

The court elaborated upon the need for a sufficiently thorough and effective investigation in various decisions, as in the case of *Assenov and Others v. Bulgaria*, in which the court held that Bulgaria had denied the applicant an effective remedy. In this case, prosecutors had failed to immediately question a series of witnesses to a police beating of a Roma adolescent in public. In addition, prosecutors at various levels had concluded, without a proper investigation, that "even if the blows were administered on the body of the juvenile, they occurred as a result of disobedience of police orders" and that the boy's father had caused the injuries.[21]

In another decision, *Aksoy v. Turkey*, the European Court of Human Rights ruled that if an applicant was in good health when detained and injured at the time of release, the burden of proof lies with the government:

> [W]here an individual is taken into police custody in good health but is found to be injured at the time of release, it is incumbent on the State to provide a plausible explanation as to the causing of injury, failing which a clear issue rises under Article 3.[22]

---

[19] Article 1 states: "The High Contracting Parties shall secure to everyone within their jurisdiction the rights and freedoms defined in Section I of this Convention." Article 3 states: "No one shall be subjected to torture or to inhuman or degrading treatment or punishment."

[20] *Assenov and Other* v. *Bulgaria* judgment, October 28, 1998, para. 102.

[21] Ibid., para. 106.

[22] *Aksoy* v. *Turkey* judgment, December 12, 1996, para 61.

Article 13 of the Convention against Torture also obliges states to ensure individuals the right to complain and to be protected against repercussions for filing a complaint.[23]

The U.N. Principles on the Effective Prevention and Investigation of Extra-legal, Arbitrary and Summary Executions encourage states to investigate all suspected cases of extra-legal, arbitrary, and summary executions. These authoritative standards explicitly include deaths in custody if there are "complaints by relatives or other reliable reports" which suggest that an unnatural death occurred. The investigation, which must be thorough, prompt, and impartial, should" determine the cause, manner and time of death, the person responsible, and any pattern or practice which may have brought about that death" and should result in a publicly available written report.[24]

---

[23] Article 13 states:
Each State Party shall ensure that any individual who alleges he has been subjected to torture in any territory under its jurisdiction has the right to complain to, and to have his case promptly and impartially examined by, its competent authorities. Steps shall be taken to ensure that the complainant and witnesses are protected against all ill-treatment or intimidation as a consequence of his complaint or any evidence given.

[24] Provision 9 of the Principles states:
There shall be thorough, prompt and impartial investigation of all suspected cases of extra-legal, arbitrary and summary executions, including cases where complaints by relatives or other reliable reports suggest unnatural death in the above circumstances. Governments shall maintain investigative offices and procedures to undertake such inquiries. The purpose of the investigation shall be to determine the cause, manner and time of death, the person responsible, and any pattern or practice which may have brought about that death. It shall include an adequate autopsy, collection and analysis of all physical and documentary evidence and statements from witnesses. The investigation shall distinguish between natural death, accidental death, suicide and homicide.

Provision 17 of the Principles states:

A written report shall be made within a reasonable period of time on the methods and findings of such investigations. The report shall be made public immediately and shall include the scope of the inquiry, procedures and methods used to evaluate evidence as well as conclusions and recommendations based on findings of fact and on applicable law. The report shall also describe in detail specific events that were found to have occurred and the evidence upon which such findings were based, and list the names of witnesses who testified, with the exception of those whose identities have been withheld for their own protection. The Government shall, within a reasonable period of time, either reply to the report of the investigation, or indicate the steps to

In Russia, the procuracy is the primary body responsible for ensuring observance of human rights, including the procedural and other rights of criminal suspects, defendants, and other detainees. However, the procuracy also plays the principal role in prosecuting crimes, as it is in charge of investigating certain categories of criminal cases and prosecutes defendants in court.

---

be taken in response to it.

THE PROCESS OF DETENTION

I'm not an object that can just be locked up, and then be content when they say sorry.

"Aslanbek Digaev"

Russian authorities began arresting men and women in connection with the renewed armed conflict in September 1999. Arrests usually followed three patterns: through identity checks at checkpoints, within Chechnya or on Chechnya's borders with other republics; as part of "mop-up" operations, immediately after Russian forces would gain military control of a community; and in other targeted sweeps of communities or households. While many of those detained were released within hours, others have been held for months–sometimes in unacknowledged incommunicado detention, and often without charge. Russian forces rarely cited any legal grounds for the detention.[25]

The pace of arrests greatly accelerated in January 2000, when General Victor Kazantsev, the commander of the United Group of Forces in Chechnya, ordered the closing Chechnya's internal borders to all men and boys between the ages of ten and sixty. Several days later, Russian authorities lifted the cross-border travel ban, but continued to limit the movement of men and boys within Chechnya, imposing a tough "identity verification regime," whereby irregularities in one's identity documents—internal passports, drivers' licenses and the like—could be grounds for suspected affiliation with Chechen fighters. General Kazantsev stated:

> [The measure] is aimed at curbing the free moving of the militants under the guise of peaceful civilians.... [Identity checks in liberated areas] plus the toughening of search procedures at checkpoints will put in very tough circumstances those who are inclined to call to arms and kill by night.[26]

A broad and arbitrary interpretation of "irregularity" was often the basis for detention for suspected rebel affiliation. Many men and women have been detained simply because they were staying in locations that were not their official, registered address; or because police questioned the authenticity of their identity documents

---

[25] For a full explanation of the failure to provide due process, see the chapter "Other Violations of the Rights of Individuals Deprived of their Liberty" below.

[26] "Russian general says movement restriction on Chechen males 'forced' measure," *Interfax News Agency/BBC Worldwide Monitoring*, January 14, 2000.

as a pretext for detention.[27] One interviewee told Human Rights Watch he was detained because his drivers' license was issued during the inter-war period. Others were detained because they share the same surname as a known Chechen commander, or because they are perceived to have relatives who are fighters. During the arrest, officers or soldiers commonly inspect the bodies of men and women for physical indications that they have been taking part in fighting, such as bruises or other marks on the shoulders (caused by the backlash of a rifle following gunfire), or calluses on the elbows, knees or hands. Often, old non-fighting related injuries formed the basis for arrest.

Arrests at Checkpoints and Border Crossings

Russian forces have established a dense network of checkpoints along major routes within Chechnya, particularly those that lead to Chechnya's borders with neighboring republics. It is not uncommon for civilians to have to clear ten or fifteen checkpoints to travel as many kilometers. Checkpoints range from heavily reinforced structures, to ad-hoc and mobile ones manned by just a few soldiers; at some checkpoints, police and soldiers use shacks, metal containers, or pits dug in the ground as improvised detention facilities. Civilians, particularly fighting-age males, often face harassment and abuse at checkpoints, and extortion is endemic.

"Issa Akhmadov," a twenty-one-year-old Grozny resident, was detained on January 19 near Znamenskoye, in northern Chechnya, after passing through about twenty checkpoints along the way from Novy Grozny, about seventy-five kilometers to the southeast. His arrest experience at the Kalaus checkpoint was typical: checkpoint police said they found a problem with his passport, would not disclose what the problem was, refused to tell his mother where they were taking him, and forbade him from speaking with her.

> My mother and sister tried to stop them, but the soldiers cocked their guns, aimed them at our mothers and said they had the right to shoot if the women crossed the barrier. On the radio, they called for a vehicle used to transport criminals. By the time the vehicle arrived, they had checked everything in our pockets, all of our papers. When I realized they wanted to detain me and take me away, I asked the soldier if I could speak to my mother.... But the soldiers refused, saying they would inform the families

---

[27]The word "propiska" has been excluded from official use since 1995 when the government introduced *registratsiya* (registration). Registration may be permanent or temporary. In everyday use people still often say "propiska" instead of "registratsiya" but do not distinguish between permanent and temporary. A Russian citizen's registered address is marked as a stamp in his or her internal passport.

The Process of Detention

themselves as there was a panic. The women were screaming, trying to do something. Two soldiers went to the barrier with their guns, to prevent the women from crossing it.[28]

At some checkpoints, the authorities cross-check passport or other information with a computerized database. However, when computers or radio links are not available, detainees sometimes remain in custody until they can be checked through the database. "Adem Hasuev," for example, was on a bus to Ingushetia when he was detained on January 17 near Znamenskoye. Checkpoint police said they suspected that "Hasuev's" passport was fake, and due to the lack of computers, he was held until February 1.

> They said that until they identified me, they would take me to Goragorskiy. Then they said they have no computer there, so they took me to Znamenskoye [about twenty-five kilometers away] the next day. They said it would take ten days because [there were so few checkpoint police] and there were many detainees.[29]

"Idris Batukaev" was arrested on December 16 at a checkpoint outside Grozny because the OMON checkpoint police said they found his date of birth and patronymic (his father's name) suspicious. He was attempting to flee the fighting and travel to Ingushetia with his family.[30] "Batukaev" was held for three days in a metal storage container at the checkpoint, during which time he was repeatedly beaten: "They beat me, shoving my shoulder into the wall so that I would have bruises there, so they could say it was from guns. They also beat me in the legs."[31]

Human Rights Watch was able to document several cases of rape at checkpoints. "Alisa Ebieva" and her sister-in-law, "Maya Selimurzaeva," were both detained, beaten, and raped at the Kavkaz border checkpoint in late January.[32] "Ebieva" told Human Rights Watch:

---

[28] Human Rights Watch interview with "Issa Akhmadov" (not his real name), aged twenty-one, Ingushetia, February 15, 2000.

[29] Human Rights Watch interview with "Adem Hasuev" (not his real name), aged twenty, Ingushetia, April 6, 2000.

[30] Human Rights Watch interview with "Idris Batukaev" (not his real name), aged twenty-seven, Ingushetia, April 26, 2000.

[31] Ibid.

[32] The Kavkaz checkpoint is located inside Chechnya, several kilometers to the east of Sleptsovsk, Ingushetia.

When my sister-in-law and I were coming back to Ingushetia, we were stopped at Kavkaz checkpoint. Instead of our passports, we had a form 9 [replacement travel document]. The photograph on the form 9 was five years old and I looked different, so the soldiers used this as an excuse. Also, my sister-in-law's name was similar to the name of a Chechen commander.[33]

"Ebieva" and "Selimurzaeva" were taken to separate metal storage containers near the checkpoint. Four Russian soldiers in "Ebieva's" container accused her of being a sniper. She told Human Rights Watch that they gave her a gun and told her to dismantle it, assemble it, and shoot, even though she reportedly never held a gun and did not know how to handle one. When she refused to handle the gun:

One soldier who was standing with his back to me punched me . . . and I fell to the floor. Two other soldiers started kicking me. I had my children's documents with me, and the soldiers told me I had given birth to many children. The soldiers told me, "You will never have children again," and beat me in the genital area.[34]

Some time later, "Maya Selimurzaeva" was brought into the metal storage container where "Ebieva" was being held. "One of these soldiers said that my sister-in-law had paid enough . . . . She had blood everywhere, her mouth was cut."[35] "Selimurzaeva" told "Ebieva" that she was raped. "Ebieva" told Human Rights Watch that she too was raped, and that she spent three months in bed recovering.

Arrests in the context of "mop-up" operations

The standard Russian strategy to gain control of Chechen communities involved heavy bombardment, the entry of ground forces, and then a "mop-up" operation to ensure that rebel fighters had been flushed out and to arrest those who remained, as well as their collaborators. During and after the "mop-up," soldiers commonly went on house-to-house passport and weapons checks.[36] They also

---

[33] Human Rights Watch interview with "Alisa Ebieva" (not her real name), age withheld, Ingushetia, March 28, 2000.
[34] Ibid.
[35] Ibid.
[36] Some mop-up operations—for example in Alkhan-Yurt and Aldi—turned into wanton rampages of summary executions and looting, with Russian forces responsible for large-scale killings and other serious abuses. Human Rights Watch, "February 5: A Day of Slaughter in Novye Aldi," a *Human Rights Watch Short Report*, vol. 12, no. 9(D), June

arbitrarily rounded up men, and on some occasions women, found in the area. Particularly vulnerable to arrest in such operations were men who were not in the village of their official, permanent residence.

For example, Russian forces detained "Khamid Taramov" during their February 3-5, 2000, sweep of Shaami Yurt because his propiska was for Grozny. "Taramov," together with eight other men, was stripped and beaten on February 4. He related his experience to Human Rights Watch:

> I was at [my parents'] home . . . it is at the edge of the village, there was a lot of work to do after the bombing, and I was in the yard. They came and asked me for my papers, they asked me why I was registered in Grozny and suggested I had come to Shaami Yurt to fight. There were about fifteen of them, they were MVD or FSK. They came in APCs.... People already taken were on buses.... On my bus we were six to eight of us altogether, two were local teachers who had retired. We were taken to the edge of the village.[37]

The men were taken to a field, where they were stripped and examined.

> We were held there approximately four hours. We were standing in dirt, there was frost and snow at that time. We had to take off our clothes. They checked our shoulders, looked for calluses on our hands. They beat us—of course they beat us. I was beaten a little, the normal way, with the butt of an automatic rifle. They kicked me several times, in the kidneys. I was almost knocked down.[38]

"Khamid Taramov" was eventually released from the field, but reported that other detainees were still missing as of May 2000. During the Shaami Yurt sweep operation on February 5, Russian forces summarily executed twenty-three-year-old Akhmed Doshaev. Villagers saw soldiers separate Doshaev and his brother, Alvi, from a group of detainees and take them under a bridge. Villagers found Doshaev's

---

2000; Human Rights Watch, "No Happiness Remains: Civilian Killings, Pillage, and Rape in Alkhan-Yurt," a *Human Rights Watch Short Report*, vol. 12, no. 5(D), April 2000.

[37]Human Rights Watch interview with "Khamid Taramov" (not his real name), aged forty-nine, Ingushetia, May 8, 2000. MVD is the Russian acronym for the Ministry of Internal Affairs; FSK is the Russian acronym for the Federal Counter-Intelligence Service, a successor to the KGB, which is now known as the FSB.

[38]Ibid.

body several weeks later.[39] Twenty-one year old Alvi Doshaev was still missing as of May 2000.[40]

"Sultan Deniev" was detained with fifteen other men in the February 7, 2000, sweep of Gekhi Chu.[41] No reasons were given for their detention. "Deniev" told Human Rights Watch that after the shelling of Gekhi Chu had ended, he emerged with his family from their basement and sought out Russian forces, fearing what would happen if Russians discovered them in their homes. The group of sixteen detainees was held "on [a] field behind the village. They started to tell us we were bandits, we did nothing for the motherland. They started to check our identity. We are all from one village, [we] never had guns. [The others,] they looked like farmers."[42] "Deniev" and the others were then transferred to Khankala, and then to Tolstoy Yurt; they were released on February 15.

In their mop-up operation of the Karpinsky district of Grozny on January 23, 2000, soldiers detained six males, including a thirteen-year-old deaf boy and two men with mental disabilities.[43] Although soldiers promised to release the six after checking their documents, one remained in custody for three months, and three others were in still in custody as of the end of May. "Leyla Saigatova" described what happened that day.

> I was in a shelter in our neighborhood and twice the soldiers came to check us. They took off the men's clothes, made them strip completely, the old as well as the young men. They checked them for callouses and...scrapes and then left. Then again they came in the afternoon, right to our basement. At that time, they took the men. I said please don't take

---

[39] Human rights watch interview with Eliza Ismailova, aged thirty, Ingushetia, April 24, 2000.

[40] Human Rights Watch interview with Tamara Doshaeva, aged forty-seven, Yandirka displaced persons camp, Ingushetia, April 28, 2000.

[41] The arrests occurred in the wake of shelling of the densely populated town: after Russian forces entered the town they executed at least seven men. See "Russian Soldiers Executed Seven Men in Chechen Village; Snipers in Gekhi-Chu Shot Civilians," Human Rights Watch press release, March 31, 2000. "Sultan Deniev" believes that the date he was detained was actually February 5 or 6, but his accounts of events in Gekhi Chu as well information from a foreign journalist who interviewed a man detained with him suggest that his date of arrest was February 7. This date was also noted on a certificate (*spravka*) given to "Sultan Deniev" upon his release.

[42] Human Rights Watch interview with "Sultan Deniev" (not his real name), aged twenty-five, Ingushetia, April 18, 2000.

[43] Although "Leyla Saigatova" and "Aslanbek Digaev" said the operation took place on January 23, another witness, Saipudin Saadulayev, gave the date as January 22.

The Process of Detention 23

them, they are our relatives, not fighters, but they took them, and said that they would be thoroughly checked and then released.[44]

"Aslanbek Digaev," whom "Saigatova" named as one of the men detained that day, was independently located by Human Rights Watch.

There was a...passport check. I have never been involved in any military operations. They came to our street, my wife and sisters were at home as well. They took six with me, all of us were with our relatives. None of them had been fighters.... When I was detained, I asked where we were going. They said they would check our documents and then be released."[45]

The men were initially taken to a military base at Solyonaia Balka, a few kilometers from the Karpinsky district. After being held there overnight, the thirteen-year-old boy was released, and the others were taken to Khankala, and then to Chernokozovo.[46]

Arrests during targeted sweeps of communities

As of this writing, Russian authorities control most of Chechnya, and perform periodic sweeps of communities under their control. These consist of house-to-house weapons searches and identity checks, ostensibly to ferret out fighters. Some of these sweep operations have followed Chechen ambushes of Russian military convoys or guerrilla-style attacks on other installations. Chechen rebels have turned almost exclusively to hit-and-run operations to carry on their military efforts against Russian forces. Human Rights Watch is concerned that arbitrary arrests of civilians will also become more commonplace.

The events in April in Serzhen Yurt illustrate this pattern. On April 24 and 26, 2000, Chechen fighters ambushed Russian convoys near Serzhen Yurt, located at the mouth of a strategic gorge.[47] Two days after the attack, Ministry of Internal

---

[44]Human Rights Watch interview with "Leyla Saigatova" (not her real name), age unknown, Ingushetia, May 11, 2000.

[45]Human Rights Watch interview with "Aslanbek Digaev" (not his real name), aged forty-two, Ingushetia, May 16, 2000.

[46]Ibid.

[47]See David Hoffman, "Russia Confirms Chechen Strike; Moscow Acknowledges Ambush Losses, Rejects Negotiations," *Washington Post*, April 28, 2000.

Affairs troops conducted a sweep during which they detained at least five men.[48] Among them was "Khamzat Vakuev," who was given no explanation before being beaten and then taken away, handcuffed, with his feet tied together. He was released several days later. He told Human Rights Watch:

> They came to my house, they checked every house on the street. It was in the morning, maybe 7:00 a.m., maybe even earlier. There were a lot of them, maybe thirty.... I was beaten with a rifle at my house, in the yard of my house. They did it with their rifle butts, it was impossible to avoid the beatings, because they beat me very hard. I was on the ground, covering my head, I just took it.... At the house I was beaten, they kicked me, and put me in handcuffs. My mother was in hysterics. They searched the house, different places, in the rooms and basements. They spent about fifteen or twenty minutes, more maybe.... They didn't ask for ID, they just beat me. They took me to a field, between Serzhen Yurt and Shali, then there they asked about papers. I said mine were at home, and they beat us.[49]

"Vakuev" was held for two days, outdoors in two separate encampments, before his relatives paid a bribe to secure his release. The other men detained with him were also released after several days.

On April 27, Russian forces conducted a sweep of Tsotsin Yurt. They surrounded one section of the village and did house-to-house searches, vandalized and looted personal property, ill-treated some villagers, and detained six men. On May 2, two of the detained men were left for dead by the side of the road, one of whom died only half an hour after he was found and brought home.[50]

---

[48]"Total of 46 tonnes of explosives seized in Chechnya," *ITAR-TASS*, April 29, 2000. Itar-Tass quoted the Ministry of Internal Affairs that the aim had been to "block and destroy a rebel group," and that raids for arms and fighters had been conducted in other places in Chechnya as well.

[49]Human Rights Watch interview with "Khamzat Vakuev" (not his real name), aged twenty-eight, May 26, 2000.

[50]Human Rights Watch interview with Tahir Turpalkhanov, aged thirty-seven, Nazran, Ingushetia, May 15, 2000. Tahir Turpalkhanov's account of events was supported by a video made by a resident of Tsotsin Yurt, who filmed some of the alleged vandalism and interviewed several witnesses as well as the surviving released detainee. See below, "Other Military Encampments" section in the "Abuse and Torture in Other Places of Detention" chapter of this report.

Russian forces also target specific individuals for arrest apart from sweep or mop-up operations. Fifty-two-year-old "Asya Arsimakova," for example, was sought out by name and arrested in the early morning hours of January 25, although Russian police failed to produce a warrant or explanation for her arrest.

> It was 6:00 a.m. I got up to pray and heard a car coming, and then as soon as I heard the car coming they knocked at the door. They jumped over the gate and surrounded our house. They said that they had been informed about us. My husband opened the door, and I was surprised, they were all masked. One said "Who is '[Asya]'?" I said "I am." They said "we came to take you, get ready." I asked him where I was being taken, and he didn't respond.... We came up to the car and they put me in it, and then they took my son. I asked why and they said, "if you don't keep quiet we'll take you all."[51]

"Arsimakova" was transferred the same day to Chernokozovo, where she was questioned about involvement in an alleged hostage exchange, and released approximately February 19 or 20 without charge.

---

[51] Human Rights Watch interview with "Asya Arsimakova" (not her real name), aged fifty-two, Ingushetia, 21 April 2000.

THE CHERNOKOZOVO DETENTION CENTER

Introduction

During January and early February 2000, the remand prison at Chernokozovo, about sixty kilometers northwest of Grozny, was the principal destination for those detained in Chechnya. It quickly became infamous for savage torture of detainees. Forms of torture included prolonged beatings, beatings to the genitals and to the soles of the feet, rape, electric shocks, tear gas, and other methods.[52] Guards also subjected detainees to profound humiliation and degrading treatment. At least one person was beaten to death. Often prison guards and other law enforcement officers would use torture to coerce confessions or testimony; just as often, however, it had no apparent purpose.

Because of the extent and severity of the allegations of abuse at Chernokozovo, Human Rights Watch carried out a detailed investigation into the facility, confirming and collaborating accounts of beatings, torture, and rape there. Human Rights Watch calls for a full investigation by the Russian authorities of what happened at Chernokozovo in January and February 2000, for those responsible for human rights violations committed there to be brought to justice, and for compensation to be granted to victims or their relatives.

Human Rights Watch independently located and conducted interviews with nineteen former detainees from Chernokozovo, including two women. In addition, the Memorial Human Rights Center, a prominent Russian group with a research presence in Ingushetia, shared with Human Rights Watch their material from interviews with other former Chernokozovo detainees. Taken together, these lengthy interviews yield a detailed picture of the abuses detainees sustained. From the time they entered the Chernokozovo facility, when Russian guards would force them to run a gauntlet of guards who would beat them mercilessly, through their stay in cramped and sordid conditions, to the time they were released, detainees had no relief from torment.

Before 1991, the prison complex at Chernokozovo had a capacity of 1,500 prisoners, possibly as a post-conviction labor colony. It fell into a state of disrepair during the interbellum years and detainees said that in January and

---

[52] The pattern of torture described below corresponds to well-documented patterns of torture throughout Russia, whereby Russian police use a combination of psychological and physical violence to disorient the individual, or reduce him or her to a state of shock so that he or she will provide any "necessary" information or sign any document. See Human Rights Watch, *Confessions at any Cost: Police Torture in Russia* (New York: Human Rights Watch, 1999).

February 2000, only part of the complex was being used.[53] It was the only detention facility operating in Chechnya at the time, with its outer perimeters guarded by Ministry of Justice employees and with Ministry of Internal Affairs employees staffing it within.[54] Eventually the Ministry of Justice established full jurisdiction over it.

It is clear, however, that the Ministry of Internal Affairs (MVD) presided over Chernokozovo from at least January 11 until early February, its most brutal phase. It is difficult to ascertain which MVD divisions were serving in the facility and perpetrating the abuse. Fearing identification and possible future retribution, Russian soldiers in Chechnya frequently wore camouflage uniforms with no division patches or pins that would identify them. However, six interviewees indicated that the Rostov OMON supplied the guards and commanded the facility during this period.[55]

Detainees described the area of the Chernokozovo prison where they were held as a single-story building, with cells along a corridor near the entrance to the building. Because guards forbade them from raising their eyes from the floor, most detainees had difficulty describing the facilities, but said that there were approximately eighteen cells along a corridor, and interrogation rooms were on the same corridor at the end of the hall. The guards had a duty room in the middle of the corridor. Other corridors branched off the hall but no detainee was able to describe where they led or what took place there. Women were held separately in at least two cells on or just off the main corridor.

Space does not permit a full description of the cramped, filthy, and sordid conditions detainees encountered in January and February 2000. Nearly every interviewee described severe overcrowding, sometimes more than thirty inmates for a cell meant for eight, often with no beds, let alone bedding. Food

---

[53]"Russia: No evidence of human rights violations found in filtration camp," RIA News Agency, Moscow, in English /BBC Worldwide Monitoring, February 29, 2000.

[54]Russia's prison system is run by the Ministry of Justice. Police lock-ups, or *izoliatry vremenogo zaderzhania* —IVS—are run by the Ministry of Internal Affairs. The deputy chief of the Ministry of Justice's Main Department for Penal Implementation, Aleksandr Zubkov, blamed the abuse at Chernokozovo in January and February on the Ministry of Internal Affairs, stating that at that time, "staff of the Justice Ministry's special unit were only responsible for guarding the perimeter and escorting prisoners." "Interior Ministry to check journalist's claims of beatings of Chechen detainees," World News Connection, February 29, 2000.

[55]OMON is the Russian acronym for special task police units, or riot police. Human Rights Watch has written to the Russian Ministry of the Interior and the procuracy to request clarification about the jurisdiction over Chernokozovo but has not received a response as of the date of publication of this report.

rations were extremely poor, there was no medical treatment, and for many there were no toilet facilities, not even a bucket in the cell. Despite the winter cold, many, if not all, of the cells were unheated.

The most serious abuse persisted at Chernokozovo for two months, even as news of it, provided by the few detainees who were able to bribe their way to liberty, began to spread. Conditions improved somewhat following the visit of a Russian "commission" during the first week of February, although many detainees were merely removed temporarily to conceal the extent of abuse. Shortly afterwards, the command of the facility rotated to another MVD division, the guards were replaced, structural improvements were made to the prison, including the addition of more cots for the detainees, and ill or injured detainees were transferred to the Naur district hospital. Detainees also noted an improvement in their treatment within the prison. As it embarked on the cleanup, Russian President Vladimir Putin's press secretary claimed that Chernokozovo was under the authority of the Ministry of Justice, although this was never formally confirmed.[56]

This "cleanup" coincided with growing international outrage at the reports of human rights violations in Chechnya, and the call by such institutions as the Council of Europe and the U.N. High Commissioner for Human Rights to send delegations to the republic. As international demand for access to Chernokozovo increased, many detainees were transferred to other facilities outside Chechnya, including regular prison facilities.

As of at least March, when the Council of Europe's Committee for the Prevention of Torture and Inhuman or Degrading Treatment or Punishment (CPT) first visited Chernokozovo, the detention facility was referred to as a pre-

---

[56] The transfer of authority can be ascertained by assessing the way Russian officials spoke of the detention facility. On February 7, officials from the Ministry of Justice said that Chernokozovo was the "only detention center in Chechnya which operates at present," which from the context seemed to imply that the facility fell under its authority. "Justice bodies supervising administering of punishments have been restored in Chechnya," ITAR-TASS, February 7, 2000. The authority of the Justice Ministry over the facility was confirmed by February 17, when Russia's spokesperson on Chechnya Sergei Yastrzhembsky said specifically that Chernokozovo fell under the Justice Ministry. Patrick Cockburn, "Russia rattled by torture claims at Chechen camps," *Independent* (London), February 18, 2000. However, when responding to allegations of the torture of Radio Liberty journalist Andrei Babitsky, the Justice Ministry said that at the time he was held, namely from mid-January until February 3, the MVD was responsible for Chernokozovo.

trial detention center (*sledstvennyi izolator*, or SIZO), which falls under the authority of the Ministry of Justice under Russian law.[57]

Beatings and other torture at Chernokozovo

From early January until the change of command in early February, detainees at Chernokozovo were subjected to constant and severe beatings and many forms of torture. Beatings began as soon as the detainees arrived at the facility, and continued throughout their stay. Some of the beatings and torture seemed to be associated with interrogations of detainees; many others appear to have be a consequence of gratuitous cruelty, vengeance, or a desire to have "fun" on the part of the guards.

The Human Corridor

When we just arrived in Chernokozovo, we were welcomed to hell, and it really was hell.[58]

All former detainees from Chernokozovo interviewed by Human Rights Watch gave very similar accounts about their arrival at the facility. They were met by a group of guards who formed a human corridor of two lines. Guards forced the detainees to run, their hands behind their heads, through this gauntlet while beating them with rubber batons, hammers, and rifle butts. Some of the guards wore masks. "Alvi Khanaev," who was brought to Chernokozovo on January 19, described this intake process:

> There were about twenty of them [guards], ten on each side. Some of them were masked, some had rubber sticks.... I was the third [to go through]. There was some officer ordering "next." Each of us had to jump out of the vehicle, put his hands behind his head with his head down, and run. As we ran through the corridor, the soldiers were

---

[57]"Visit by the European Committee for the Prevention of Torture to the North Caucasian Region of the Russian Federation," CPT Press Release, March 6, 2000. Furthermore, two detainees interviewed by Human Rights Watch who were released on March 30 were given virtually identical, handwritten certificates stating that they had been held in "investigative isolation" at IZ 4/12 Chernokozovo (although both had actually been transferred to other facilities). Human Rights Watch interviews with "Issa Habuliev" (not his real name), aged forty-six, Ingushetia, April 8, 2000; and "Movsar Larsanov," Ingushetia, May 25, 2000.

[58]Former detainee to Human Rights Watch, February 21, 2000.

kicking us and beating us with rubber sticks and whatever they had in their hands.[59]

"Alimkhan Visaev," who arrived at Chernokozovo in late January, gave a very similar account of the scene: "We were ordered to run down the corridor with our hands behind our head. The soldiers were standing in two lines outside. We had to run through them, being hit with batons and kicked."[60] When twenty-one-year-old "Issa Akhmadov" arrived at Chernokozovo in early January, the corridor was not yet ready, and so detainees were beaten as it was being prepared:

> We were kept [waiting] for twenty minutes.... We learned later that they were preparing the corridor from the vehicle to the jail. About fifteen or twenty soldiers were standing in two lines, with their rubber sticks. When each of us stepped out [of the vehicle], the soldier pushed us with his gun. They then beat us with rubber night sticks and made us lay down. Then one [soldier] asked whether the corridor was ready. Others replied that it was, and we were ordered one by one to run through to the building. When I was running through the corridor, each soldier hit me with his stick.[61]

At least one person, thirty-two year-old Aindi Kovtorashvilli, died from beatings while "running the corridor." According to his relatives, Kovtorashvilli had a serious shrapnel wound to his head when he was detained on January 11 in Tolstoy-Yurt. After a three-week search for Kovtorashvilli, an aunt finally located his body at the morgue at the Mozdok military base.[62]

Human Rights Watch interviewed separately three men who were transported with Kovtorashvilli from Tolstoy-Yurt to Chernokozovo and who witnessed the beating that appeared to kill him. "Abdul Jambekov" related to Human Rights Watch how Kovtorashvilli died January 11, soon after their arrival in Chernokozovo:

---

[59]Human Rights Watch interview with "Alvi Khanaev" (not his real name), aged thirty-nine, Ingushetia, February 17, 2000.

[60]Human Rights Watch interview with "Alimkhan Visaev" (not his real name), aged twenty-seven, Ingushetia, March 22, 2000.

[61]Human Rights Watch interview with "Issa Akhmadov," Ingushetia, February 15, 2000.

[62]Human Rights Watch interview with Tanya Kovtorashvilli, Nazran, Ingushetia, April 13, 2000.

> His name was Aindi, I do not know his surname. He was wounded, he had shrapnel in his head and couldn't talk. We only spent several hours on the bus while riding from Tolstoy-Yurt. I don't know anything else about him. He was in front of me on the bus. They called out his name, but he was like a small child because of his injuries and someone needed to help him.
>
> So I tried to help him, and then one guy with a mask said "I said, one by one," and because I tried to go with him they struck me, then they started beating him. Then it was my turn.... They just pulled him like a dust broom and just threw his body away, in front of us. It was useless even trying to bandage him, he was dead.[63]

"Issa Habuliev" told Human Rights Watch that he was transported from Tolstoy-Yurt to Chernokozovo on January 11 with Kovtorashvilli, whom he identified only as a man with a Georgian last name and a gangrenous head wound. According to "Habuliev," "He was wounded, but while crossing the gauntlet they continued to beat him. He died right there, he was right next to me."

A third witness who had arrived on the same bus from Tolstoy-Yurt confirmed the death of Kovtarashvilli:

> [A man] who was wounded, they beat him on the head, so that he died. He was about 180 [centimeters tall].... He was in the first group to come out of the bus. He had an open wound on his head, he was confused, he didn't understand anything. He had received one blow on the place on his head where he was injured, he fell down and then three more guys [guards] came and surrounded him and started to violently beat him. When I looked at him he was bleeding, there was a puddle of blood around him.... When I came through [the gauntlet] he was still alive, they said to stand up but he couldn't, and that is why they got angry and then constantly beat him.[64]

---

[63] Human Rights Watch interview with "Abdul Jambekov" (not his real name), aged thirty-three, Ingushetia, May 7, 2000.

[64] Human Rights Watch interview with "Magomed Kantiev" (not his real name), aged forty-four, Ingushetia, May 13, 2000.

When Kovtorashvilli's aunt saw the body at the morgue she noted that, "My nephew had a hole in his head. His hands had been fractured, and on the body there were traces of beatings."[65]

"Fatimah Akhmedova," a female detainee at Chernokozovo, witnessed the brutal beating of a retarded fourteen-year-old boy when she arrived at Chernokozovo on February 1. After she was allowed to walk through the corridor of soldiers without being beaten, the soldiers called for the young boy:

> I heard the soldiers say, "You brought us a clown here, let the clown go next," referring to the fourteen-year-old. I started to explain that he really could not comprehend what was happening, and asked [the soldiers] not to beat him. Then I looked back and I saw the soldiers putting on their masks. They started to beat the boy with batons, and they kicked him. The boy screamed, calling for his mother and asking for God's help. [He] was beaten for an hour. He was bleeding from the mouth, and had a head injury and was having trouble breathing. Then, when the boy was laying flat on the ground, they kicked him and said, "Why are you bleeding? Stand up!" Then I fainted, and a soldier took me to the doctor.[66]

Torture in the Context of Interrogations

Prisoners taken for interrogation were beaten and tortured, both on the way to interrogation and, according to some, during questioning in the interrogation room itself. Beatings prior to questioning were aimed at "softening up" a suspect to encourage compliance during questioning. Guards and interrogators also sought to humiliate detainees, forcing them to crawl into interrogation rooms and to address staff with abject humility. Torture worsened at night, when many interrogations seemed to take place and when the guards utterly ran amok. While in some cases documented by Human Rights Watch beatings did not take place during interrogations, case investigators probably had knowledge of their occurrence and took no effective action to prevent them or punish the perpetrators.

---

[65] Human Rights Watch interview with Tanya Kovtorashvilli, Nazran, Ingushetia, April 13, 2000. Initially, the morgue attendants demanded money for the release of the body, saying, "If you will pay for him, we will give you the body back." After a lengthy argument, the aunt was finally allowed to leave with Aindi Kovtorashvilli's body after paying 800 rubles for the "treatment" of the corpse.

[66] Human Rights Watch interview with "Fatimah Akhmedova" (not her real name), aged twenty-two, Ingushetia, March 7, 2000.

According to multiple Human Rights Watch interviewees, questioning took place in two rooms located at the end of the main corridor of prison cells. As is standard practice elsewhere in Russia, prisoners were forbidden to look up as they walked along the corridor. Guards, some wearing masks, forbade prisoners from making eye contact with them. Detainees were sometimes called for multiple questioning, and thus were subjected to beatings and other abuse several times.[67] Guards also meted out beatings as they took prisoners to locations within the facility other than the interrogation room.

Several detainees said that guards tortured them during interrogations in an attempt to force them to give information, confess, or sign a statement or other documents prepared by the authorities. "Abdul Jambekov" was interrogated, beaten, and humiliated in Chernokozovo, where he was detained from January 11 until February 18:

> They took me from the cell, asked me when I was arrested and for certain facts. They read me the interrogation report and I signed it, because it was my own words. Then they brought me the warrant for my arrest, and I refused to sign that. They started to beat me, and said that they would shoot me if I didn't sign. There were four of them, two behind me and two in front. Those sitting had no ID, but those walking around had badges on. They beat me with truncheons and sticks, also with iron tubes. They did this whenever you didn't answer their question. There were two guys behind me, they had masks on, and they were ready, just waiting to beat you if you didn't answer their questions. They wanted me to sign a piece of paper. I asked if it was possible to read, even to look at the papers that I was supposed to sign but they didn't let me. They said I should just sign it."[68]

"Jambekov" also described the humiliation guards subjected him to:

> They would make us say "Comrade Colonel, let me crawl to you" but he wasn't a colonel, that was just his dream. After they beat us, they

---

[67]Thirty-eight-year-old "Aslanbek Digaev," for example told Human Rights Watch that he "was taken for official questioning four times," and that when taken for questioning he had to run, head down, with guards beating him. Human Rights Watch interview with "Aslanbek Digaev," Ingushetia, May 16, 2000.

[68]Human Rights Watch interview with "Abdul Jambekov," Ingushetia, May 7, 2000.

made us say "thank you," and if you couldn't even stand then they would still make you say "thank you" and crawl away.[69]

As of early May, "Jambekov" still suffered from the medical consequences of the beatings in detention. According to his mother, X-rays taken in April revealed three broken ribs, and the doctor's diagnoses also included prolapsed kidneys, problems with his liver, and an irregular heartbeat. She also reported that "Jambekov" had developed a stammer and has other neurological ailments (confusion, headaches), which his doctor attributed to beatings sustained to the head.[70]

Guards at Chernokozovo often focused their beatings on the testicles of male inmates, causing excruciating pain and long-term health problems for their victims. According to "Yakub Tasuev," "They asked if I was married or not. If someone was unmarried, they said 'You will never have children,' and kicked them [in the testicles]."[71] "Sultan Eldarbiev" told Human Rights Watch that on February 7, as he was being taken for questioning around 10:00 or 11:00 p.m., he saw guards beating two men in the genital area:

> I saw a man during questioning, crouched naked with his hands over his head. I turned and saw [another] naked man. Two men [guards] separated his legs. [Another man] tried to force him to sign a [confession] saying he was a fighter, cut off heads, traded in people. They kicked down on his genitals, saying "You will sign it! You will sign it!"[72]

Human Rights Watch located and interviewed separately the man whom "Sultan Eldarbiev" saw being kicked in that incident. "Ali Baigiraev," aged thirty-four, described how guards took him from his cell late at night on February 7, and openly discussed whether or not to rape him before administering a brutal beating:

---

[69] Ibid.

[70] Human Rights Watch interview with "Marina Jambekova" (not her real name) Ingushetia, May 28, 2000.

[71] Human Rights Watch interview with "Yakub Tasuev" (not his real name), aged thirty-two, Ingushetia, February 21, 2000.

[72] Human Rights Watch interview with "Sultan Eldarbiev" (not his real name), aged forty-four, Ingushetia, March 25, 2000.

> It was February 7, late at night. I was lying on the floor, two guards held my legs while another kicked me in the testicles. I would lose consciousness and come to, I lost consciousness four times. They hit me around the head, there was blood. They would beat me unconscious and wait until I came round: "He's woken up," and they would come in and beat me [again].[73]

"Baigiraev" lost a testicle as a result of injuries sustained during the February 7 beatings. He was still recovering in the hospital, more than two months after the beating, when he was interviewed by Human Rights Watch.[74]

According to "Baigiraev," the second man mentioned by "Sultan Eldarbiev" was a twenty-seven-year-old man from Staraia Sunzha district of Grozny: "I didn't understand [at the time] what was happening, but I saw this naked man. I saw guards holding the man on a chair, and he was screaming like he was being castrated. He told me later that they held his testicles with pliers, and beat him there with batons."[75]

Thirty-two-year-old "Ibrahim Aziev" told Human Rights Watch that guards beat his feet during interrogation on January 21:

> When I was taken for questioning, the investigator tried to force me to sign a confession, this happened on my second day at Chernokozovo [January 21]. On the way to, during, and on the way back from questioning I was beaten with rubber sticks on my shoulders and back. [Then] they made me lie on the ground, with my feet raised, and beat the soles of my feet. They wanted me to sign an article 208 confession, saying I participated in the fighting.[76]

"Ibrahim Aziev" was unable to walk for two weeks after his release because of the pain caused by the falanga beatings.

---

[73] Human Rights Watch interview with "Ali Baigiraev" (not his real name), aged thirty-four, Ingushetia, February 21, 2000.

[74] Baigiraev described how he experienced *falanga* torture when being questioned on February 5, 2000: "I was beaten and kicked on the soles of my feet with metal and plastic batons, reversed to beat me on the soles of my feet [with the metal part]." Ibid.

[75] Ibid.

[76] Human Rights Watch interview with "Ibrahim Aziev" (not his real name), aged thirty-two, Ingushetia, March 2, 2000.

Thirty-two-year-old "Yakub Tasuev" also told Human Rights Watch how he had experienced falanga torture at Chernokozovo in early February:

> They used the iron part of their sticks [batons] to beat me on the bottom of my feet. They put a cloth in my mouth so I couldn't scream, and they handcuffed me. They made me lay down on my stomach with my head under the table. They took off my boots and socks, and beat my soles, especially on the heels. Then they made me stand against the wall with my hands up, lifted my shirt and beat me on the kidneys with the sticks.... These beatings took place mostly in the interrogation room, but also in the corridor on the way to interrogation.[77]

"Sultan Eldarbiev" told Human Rights Watch that one of the men in his cell, a twenty-five-year-old man from the Karpinsky district of Grozny, was beaten so badly on his feet that he could no longer walk: "He couldn't walk, he had been beaten on the soles of his feet and had broken ribs. His feet were black and he had open wounds on the soles of his feet."[78]

Several detainees said that electric shocks were used during the interrogations. According to "Umar Khakimov," who was held in Chernokozovo from February 5 to 12:

> They also used electric power, they made you touch the wires. They just give you the wires and you are not allowed to see what it is, you just have to grab it. When I touched the wires, I felt like my eyes were going to pop out. This was in the interrogation room. They made you stand with your hands up. Two soldiers hold you from behind and make you touch the wires. They shocked me like this once. After the interrogation, they took me back to my cell. I was unable to walk out because of the pain, and had to crawl back.[79]

"Sultan Eldarbiev" was also subjected to electric shock:

---

[77] Human Rights Watch interview with "Yakub Tasuev," Ingushetia, February 21, 2000.

[78] Human Rights Watch interview with "Sultan Eldarbiev," Ingushetia, March 25, 2000.

[79] Human Rights Watch interview with "Umar Khakimov" (not his real name), aged forty-six, Ingushetia, February 21, 2000.

> They tried to make me sign confessions that we were *wahhabis*,[80] fighters, that we were supporting the fighters. I did not sign. They used electric shock to make me sign, but I did not do it. I was forced to put my back to the wall. Two guards stood next to me, my hands were on my head. There were two cables, and they held the cables to my body. I felt I was going crazy, I fell unconscious once. I was afraid my heart would stop beating. They splashed water in my face. Two or three times during the interrogation, they shocked me.[81]

"Alimkhan Visaev," detained in Chernokozovo for eighteen days from late January and early February, was brutally beaten during interrogation the first day he was transferred to Chernokozovo:

> The interrogator was in camouflage, he was a high-ranking officer.... When my name was called, I had to leave the cell with my hands behind my head until the guard locked the cell. I was then brought to the interrogation room, while the soldier accompanying me beat me with his rubber stick. When I entered the interrogation room, I was ordered to sit on a chair. I was asked whether I was a fighter, and where I was hiding weapons.
>
> There were two guards, one on each side and the interrogator behind his desk facing me. One guard had a gun, the other had a baton. They would ask questions and I would reply, the interrogator then would say,

---

[80] In Russia and Central Asia, the term "Wahhabism" refers to "Islamic fundamentalism" and extremism. Discrepancy exists among the definitions of "Wahhabism," however. Historically, "Wahhabism" is a branch of Sunnism practiced in Saudi Arabia and named after its founder, Islamic scholar Muhammad ibn 'Abd al-Wahhab. The eighteenth-century movement known as "Wahhabism" advocated a conservative agenda of purifying the Muslim faith and simultaneously encouraged independent thinking, a potentially liberal stance.

The term is used in Russia and Central Asia to suggest radicalism and militancy. It is often used pejoratively. The Russian and Central Asian conception of "Wahhabism" retains a linkage to "foreignness" in general, including to Saudi Arabia. In the context of the Chechnya war, Russian soldiers and many Chechen civilians use the term "Wahhabi" broadly and derogatively to refer to Chechen fighters, particularly those who serve under Khattab, a field commander from the Middle East known for his religious agenda in Chechnya.

[81] Human Rights Watch interview with "Sultan Eldarbiev," Ingushetia, March 25, 2000.

> "Answer now!" and the soldiers were beating me. I was hit with the rifle butt on my neck, with a bat on my back, and [they] hit me on the head, shoulders and ribs with the baton.
>
> I was interrogated for a half hour or more. When I said, "No I'm not a fighter," they said, "Now you'll remember," and beat me. The interrogation room had concrete walls, three meters wide and four meters long, with a chair and a desk for the interrogator and a chair for the detainee. I was taken for interrogation three of four times, with the same questions and the same beatings, but different interrogators. I saw the interrogator's face, but the guards wore masks.[82]

"Issa Akhmadov" was interrogated first on January 17, the day he was transferred to Chernokozovo.

> I noticed it was getting dark. I made my evening and night prayers. Just as I finished, I was called out again. As I stepped out of the cell, I was struck in the back of the neck and fell to the floor. They ordered me to crawl along the corridor, which was twenty meters long. I tried to crawl and one of the soldiers was kicking me in the kidney, and another in the shoulder. A third was walking behind me, with a gun pointing at me. This way I was made to crawl through the corridor and enter the investigator's office.[83]

During questioning "Akhmadov" was accused of being a fighter:

> They asked me what fighters I knew, I said I had seen Basayev and others on TV but did not know any fighters myself. Then the interrogator told the soldiers to take me away. It lasted about twenty minutes. On the way back to the cell, I was beaten again by three soldiers. They beat me against the wall, threw me against the floor and beat me on the head. I was put back in the cell and the next one was taken.[84]

---

[82] Human Rights Watch interview with "Alimkhan Visaev," Ingushetia, March 22, 2000.

[83] Human Rights Watch interview with "Issa Akhmadov," Ingushetia, February 15, 2000.

[84] Ibid.

The Chernokozovo Detention Center

The day after his interrogation, "Akhmadov" and his cellmates were ordered to leave their cell for a security check. In the corridor, the men were forced to walk through a gauntlet of guards, one of whom struck Akhmadov with a hammer, causing him pain for months. He described the incident to Human Rights Watch:

> They were checking the jail to see if we were trying to escape. They made us run to the cold room...with fifteen soldiers beating us there and back. Among the soldiers were two with big metal [sledge] hammers. When I was running from the cell to the cold room, I was struck by the hammer on my backbone, and on the way back I was struck on my leg. The other men that were there with me had ribs broken, shoulder blades broken, or a knee broken.[85]

When interviewed by Human Rights Watch almost one month after this incident, "Akhmadov" still bore the signs of the injury. He walked with extreme difficulty, and was on strong painkillers to control his constant back pain. His cellmate, twenty-year-old "Adem Hasuev," independently described the same incident.[86]

"Movsar Larsanov," detained in Chernokozovo from mid-January until March 1, noted that he was beaten and humiliated as he was taken to and from the interrogation room, but not during questioning.

> As soon as you would leave the cell, they would beat you, they would shout at you the whole time. As soon as you came to the room...first they would beat you and then you would have to lie down on the floor and crawl to them. You would have to say, "Request permission to crawl." Me personally, they beat me on the knees, with clubs, and on the kidneys. They kicked me in the chest [and I fell]. I stood up and they beat me again, they kicked me in the chest and said stand up, and again, and again, and again, until I couldn't stand up any more.[87]

"Akhmed Isaev," held in Chernokozovo from January 19 to 30, had a very similar experience that confirmed the practice described by "Larsanov." He was beaten on the way to and from interrogation, but the case investigator, whom he described as a man with a reddish beard, did not harm him:

---

[85] Ibid.
[86] Human Rights Watch interview with "Adem Hasuev," Ingushetia, April 6, 2000.
[87] Human Rights Watch interview with "Movsar Larsanov," Ingushetia, May 25, 2000

[On January 19], we were taken for interrogation one by one. When the door was opened and somebody was called out, he had to step out of the cell, fall on his knees, put his hand behind his head and face against the wall. Two or three guards were beating us. They were wearing masks and did not let us look into their eyes. I was shown the opened door which was about fifteen meters away. I was ordered to fall down and crawl.

They ordered me...when I reached the door, to...say the words, "Citizen Officer, thank you for seeing me. I am [gives name]. According to your order, I have crawled up here." They also said that the faster I would crawl, the less hits I would get. They laughed, saying I crawled like a "Wahhabi."

I reached the door, entered the room, and one guard beat me with an iron rod.... The interrogation lasted about forty minutes. I was beaten when I entered the room, and when it was over. There were two people in the room, and two guards outside the room. The one who asked the questions had a knitted cap and reddish beard. Each of us had been interrogated and then sent to a different cell.[88]

Like Isaev, "Alvi Khanaev," was brought to Chernokozovo on January 19 and said he was questioned by a man with a reddish beard who did not harm him. He also was beaten before being interrogated, and was forced to strip before the questioning began, which he said took place at 5:00 a.m. "Khanaev" stressed to Human Rights Watch that he remained stripped of his clothes during the interrogation, but that "[the prosecutor's] attitude towards me was not one of animosity." At the end of the questioning, "Khanaev" begged the investigator to ask the guards not to beat him on the way back to the cell. The investigator's secretary indicated to the guards not to harm Khanaev, but they beat him and the other men on the way to the cell anyway.[89]

Night Beatings: "They were out of control"[90]
At night guards at Chernokozovo were apparently given free reign for wanton abuse and humiliation. It was then that the most brutal treatment

---

[88] Human Rights Watch interview with "Akhmed Isaev" (not his real name), aged twenty-four, Ingushetia, February 17, 2000.
[89] Human Rights Watch interview with "Alvi Khanaev," Ingushetia, February 17, 2000.
[90] "Issa Habuliev," describing the nighttime beatings in Chernokozovo.

occurred. Many detainees noted that the playing of loud music would signal the start of the "night time regime," when guards, often inebriated, would conducted mock interrogations, during which they would mete out severe beatings or other forms of torture to those who did not comply. They would also force detainees to engage in humiliating acts. "Magomed Habuev," reflecting on the nighttime regime, commented, "During the day, you might be beaten with clubs, but at night, there was no way to be able to deal with that kind of torture."[91]

"Ali Baigiraev"described being brutally beaten at night, during which time he said beatings were more severe than those during the day. On the night of February 7:

> It was a beating, not an interrogation. They took me out of the cell, I don't know how many there were. Three or four were beating me with sticks and kicking me. By the time I reached the interrogation room, I was already very weak. When I entered the room, there were about ten people. They didn't ask any questions, they started beating me. They beat me, beat me, beat me, and I fell down. Only after I fell down did they start asking questions. But you have no strength to answer, because they put you against the wall and start beating you again.
>
> They beat me on the head, saying I was very strong. Then they banged my head against the wall. The last time I regained consciousness, I started sitting up and I saw the feet of the soldiers, and they said, "He's coming to. They asked me if I had children. I said I did and they answered, "You won't have any more," and they kicked me in my private parts. Then I lost consciousness again. I didn't regain consciousness, I just heard them saying, "Let's drag him into the cell." They ordered me to stand up but I couldn't. They dragged me into the cell. My jacket and hat remained in the interrogation room and I never got them back.[92]

"Aslanbek Digaev," detained from January 25 until February 18 in Chernokozovo, showed a Human Rights Watch researcher a scar on his head that extended from the level of his ear up towards the crown of his head, the result, he said, of a blow from the butt of a rifle which he received during a nighttime mock interrogation.

---

[91]Human Rights Watch Interview with "Magomed Habuev," Ingushetia, May 13, 2000.
[92]Human Rights Watch interview with "Ali Baigiraev," Ingushetia, February 21, 2000

There was also unofficial "questioning," when they were drunk, in the same interrogation rooms, with no papers. They would act as if they were generals. I [can't count] the number of times I was taken for "unofficial questioning." At 7:00 p.m., they turned on the music, and it lasted until morning. I have scars on my head, my nose and ribs were broken. [My head] was bleeding.... They were maniacs, they enjoyed it.[93]

Humiliating "games"

At night, primarily, guards played abusive "games" with the prisoners. Many detainees described being forced to perform humiliating acts for guards, often when the guards were drunk. Guards rode on top of "Aslanbek Digaev" while he was on his hands and knees. He described this to Human Rights Watch, "They forced us to kneel down, in the corridor, and sat on top of us, and would act as if they were in a car. They played these kinds of games in the corridor."[94]

"Abdul Jambekov" also reported being forced by guards to participate in humiliating "games":

They also had a separate room, it was covered with blood, at the end of the hall. There were some broken chairs in there. They rode people there, sitting on top of them, beating them with clubs. They made me crawl, saying that I would have to crawl such a distance in such a time. If not, then you had to do it again. We were taken there one by one, they beat me, and others.[95]

Describing this humiliation, "Jambekov" became visibly distressed and physically agitated.

Others described how the guards forced them to run up and down the corridor; if the guards were not satisfied with the speed, they made the detainee repeat the exercise.[96] Another interviewee described how guards piled detainees on top of each other in the corridor, so that they were laying across each other two by two. The guards then beat them when this "tower" collapsed.[97]

---

[93] Human Rights Watch interview with "Aslanbek Digaev," Ingushetia, May 16, 2000.
[94] Ibid.
[95] Human Rights Watch interview with "Abdul Jambekov," Ingushetia, May 7, 2000.
[96] Human Rights Watch interview with "Movsar Larsanov," Ingushetia, March 25, 2000.
[97] Human Rights Watch interview with "Asya Arsimakova," Ingushetia, April 21, 2000.

The Chernokozovo Detention Center

Another form of torture which was reportedly administered at Chernokozovo was the application of a heated brick to the body of detainees. Forty-four-year-old "Magomed Kantiev" told Human Rights Watch that guards had burned him with heated bricks on his back on several occasions:

> I was forced to strip to the waist, and lie on the floor. Then the guards would put an ordinary house brick which they had heated with a lamp on my back, and another soldier would stand on the brick. I was subjected to this on numerous occasions. Whether the brick left burns depended on how much it had been heated. At some point I had blisters on my back.... Day by day, they get better. But there are still psychological scars, they will not heal.[98]

Physical Exhaustion

Most former detainees reported that they were forced to stand in exhausting positions, such as with their hands above their heads facing a wall, for extended periods of time, sometimes for an entire day. Guards beat those who failed to sustain this position. At least two of those interviewed indicated that rather than put their hands against the wall, they were ordered to stand facing the wall with their palms facing backwards.[99]

Guards regularly checked cells to make sure detainees were standing in the ordered positions. According to "Akhmed Isaev":

> At 6:00 a.m., we were woken up, sometimes earlier. We were allowed to go to bed at 11:00 p.m. We had to stand the whole day long. The cell was very small, and when the guards looked through the peep hole they could not see one corner. We took turns going to this corner to get some rest. We had to face the wall and keep our hands up, the whole day.[100]

"Alvi Khanaev" confirmed that those who could not endure standing attempted to hide in the corner. "Naturally, from time to time we dropped our

---

[98]Human Rights Watch interview with "Magomed Kantiev," Ingushetia, May 13, 2000.
[99]Human Rights Watch interview with Andrei Babitsky, May 24, 2000; Human Rights Watch interview with "Movsar Larsanov," May 25, 2000.
[100]Human Rights Watch interview with "Akhmed Isaev," Ingushetia, February 17, 2000.

hands, because it was impossible to stand like this, although we knew we would be punished."[101]

Guards punished not only those who dropped their arms, but sometimes also the entire cell. "Adem Hasuev" told Human Rights Watch: "Sometimes, you get tired and drop your hands, in this case, they beat everyone."[102] According to "Alimkhan Visaev," "[t]he soldiers watched us through the peep hole. If we dropped our hands or sat down, we would be taken out and beaten. One man [from Grozny], sat down once, he was taken out and beaten brutally."[103]

"Ali Baigiraev" and his cellmates were forced to stand as a punishment, after one of them had been examined by a visiting Russian delegation on February 9 or 10. "They made all the people in the cell stand with their hands up all night. But I couldn't stand on [any] feet, so the others were ordered to keep us standing, otherwise they would also be beaten, all of them."[104]

Prison guards frequently used teargas in the cells of detainees, causing coughing fits and breathing problems for the unprotected inmates. Eight detainees, including Radio Liberty correspondent Andrei Babitsky, confirmed the use of teargas at Chernokozovo in interviews with Human Rights Watch. Twenty-four-year old "Akhmed Isaev" (not his real name) explained: "They asked us if we wanted to smoke, and when someone went to the door to take the cigarettes they would spray teargas inside instead of [giving] the cigarettes. They did this about six different times."[105]

At other times, guards used teargas to punish detainees when they violated the rigid rules of the facility. One detainee related how his cell was sprayed with teargas when the detainees could no longer endure the physical demands placed upon them: "They would do this when someone let down their hands or sat down. The guard would open the peephole and say, 'Hah, you are sitting down, now I'm going to get you,' and spray the gas."[106]

---

[101]Human Rights Watch interview with "Alvi Khanaev," Ingushetia, February 17, 2000.

[102]Human Rights Watch interview with "Adem Hasuev," Ingushetia, April 6, 2000.

[103]Human Rights Watch interview with "Alimkhan Visaev," Ingushetia, March 22, 2000.

[104]Human Rights Watch interview with "Ali Baigiraev," Ingushetia, February 21, 2000.

[105]Human Rights Watch interview with "Akhmed Isaev," Ingushetia, February 17, 2000. Another witness confirmed this practice. "Umar Khakimov" told Human Rights Watch: "They used gas. They asked if we wanted to smoke, and then used the teargas." Human Rights Watch interview, Ingushetia, February 21, 2000.

[106]Human Rights Watch interview with "Alvi Khanaev," Ingushetia, February 17, 2000.

Rape

Reports of rape at Chernokozovo emerged, despite the strong taboo in Chechen culture against revealing instances of sexual assault. Chechnya's Muslim culture and national traditions strictly regulate relations between men and women, and inappropriate behavior is subject to severe and often violent sanctions. Unmarried women who have been raped are unlikely to be able to marry, and married women who are raped are likely to be divorced by their husbands. In the patriarchal and homophobic Chechen society, rape and sexual assault of men is particularly difficult to discuss. Yet more than half of those interviewed by Human Rights Watch alleged that guards raped and sexually assaulted male and female detainees at Chernokozovo, although these allegations require further confirmation. Although none of the interviewees explicitly stated that he or she was a victim of rape, several did describe abuse rising to the level of sexual assault and provided credible evidence of rape in the facility.

Some women were forced to strip in front of the male guards. "Fatimah Akhmedova" described to Human Rights Watch one incident of forced nudity during an interrogation at Chernokozovo:

> On the first day of February at around midnight or so, I was called out for questioning. They forced me to strip and [accused me of being a fighter or sniper]. I was questioned by eight people, three were doctors in military uniforms, two of those [doctors] were brought to me when I was sick. I was stripped only for questioning. I saw all of them, one looked like an Uzbek. They questioned me for one half hour, they shouted and swore at me, that if I didn't tell the truth they would keep me there until I died. I was taken out once on [February 1] and three times on the second day.

Male prisoners also reported incidents of forced nudity, usually in the context of severe torture to the genital area.[107] Sexual violence in the form of forced nudity served to inflict psychological humiliation upon detainees, and added to Chernokozovo's environment of terror and intimidation.[108] Forced

---

[107] See below, specifically Human Rights Watch interview with "Sultan Eldarbiev," Ingushetia, March 25, 2000.

[108] The Trial Chamber in the *Akayesu* case defined sexual violence broadly: "Sexual violence is not limited to physical invasion of the human body and may include acts which do not involve penetration or even physical contact," including forced nudity. *Akayesu Judgment*, ICTR-96-4-T.

nudity also served as a precursor to additional sexual violence described by male and female detainees.

"Alvi Khanaev," who was transferred to Chernokozovo on January 19, reported that one woman arrested with him was raped the first night they spent at Chernokozovo.

> The woman that was with us in the vehicle [name withheld] was forty-two years old and has four children, she is from Tolstoy-Yurt. That evening, when men were interrogated, that woman was beaten mercilessly. Judging from the noise, I could guess that she was being beaten with the rubber sticks, she was beaten. She was beaten for ten or fifteen minutes, with some pauses of one or two minutes. Then, for half an hour we didn't hear her at all. We could hear everything that was going on in the jail, but could not see everything. In half an hour, we understood that she had been raped. The soldiers were using bad language and this lasted for about thirty minutes. Then everything stopped.

Human Rights Watch was unable to confirm independently this or several other accounts of rape of women. The difficulties inherent in documenting such abuse are enormous. In the patriarchal and homophobic Chechen society, speaking of rape and sexual assault is taboo. Women detainees may have feared to admit that any of the women were raped in the facility, aware of the social stigma and shame associated with rape.

Human Rights Watch did gather detailed testimony relating to physical evidence of anal rape of men in Chernokozovo. "Ibrahim Aziev" claimed that his cellmate told him that he had been raped on January 23, the day before Aziev arrived at Chernokozovo. Aziev described the victim as young, about fifteen years old, and attractive. "When I saw him, he was just like a corpse. He was breathing, but nothing more. They didn't take him again while I was there. He said he was raped, those were his words."[109]

"Sultan Eldarbiev," held in Chernokozovo from February 5 until February 11, said that a man from his cell was sodomized with a truncheon.

> They raped with a baton a thirty-two or thirty-three-year-old, [name withheld]. When he was brought round, he was brought to our cell

---

[109] Human Rights Watch interview with "Ibrahim Aziev," Ingushetia, March 2, 2000, and April 17, 2000.

naked, with his clothes in his hands. There was dried blood leading from his anus, he didn't sign [a confession]. I was in cell 16.[110]

"Ali Baigiraev," who was held in the same cell with "Sultan Eldarbiev," and who had been severely beaten in the genitals, was himself threatened with rape:

> I heard the soldiers say while they were kicking me on the floor, "Let's fuck him." Then they said "Let's not dirty ourselves" (*Ne budem pachkatsia*). When I was taken for "questioning" I was beaten and they said "Let's fuck him." "Let's question him," I was taken from the cell, and by the time I got to the questioning room, I was already only half-conscious. I was taken from this room to another where they said they would fuck me.[111]

Several interviewees said that guards gave male rape victims a woman's name as a nickname, and teased them later about the rape. "Alvi Khanaev" told Human Rights Watch that on several occasions he heard guards tease and beat men in the corridor. He described one incident that began with guards ordering the victim out of his cell:

> You could hear everything. Then the soldiers ordered him to undress. Then... something was done to him, [sodomy]. We heard him say, "please, please, don't!" This continued for about five minutes. After all this happened, the victim said, "You have killed me." They renamed him Alla, they said, "From now on, you will be Alla, a woman."[112]

Possibly describing the same incident, "Alimkhan Visaev" said that his cellmate had been raped during the last week of January or the first week of February.

> They took one of the men from my cell and raped him. They gave him a nickname, Tania or Natasha. He was about twenty years old.... They raped him and threw him into our cell, and the next day they took him

---

[110]Human Rights Watch interview with "Sultan Eldarbiev," Ingushetia, March 25, 2000.
[111]Human Rights Watch interview with "Ali Baigiraev," Ingushetia, March 25, 2000.
[112]Human Rights Watch interview with "Alvi Khanaev," Ingushetia, February 17, 2000

to a different cell. The man cried "It hurts, it hurts, don't do it....You have killed me."[113]

The "Cleanup"

As international attention focused on the human rights violations in Chechnya, intergovernmental organizations—particularly the Council of Europe—began to pressure Russia to accept official visiting delegations to the region. At about the same time, Russian authorities orchestrated a cleanup of Chernokozovo. Clearly aware by this time that inmates were being tortured, the authorities improved somewhat the physical conditions, and by February 10, ensured that the guards who had perpetrated the worst abuses were rotated out. At the same time, Moscow authorities vehemently denied any abuse had taken place in Chernokozovo, and delayed the international community's access to the facility. Improvements, at first, were cosmetic, and inmates were merely taken out temporarily to conceal from the first round of visitors the degree of overcrowding and to hide some of the inmates who had been severely abused. This pattern was repeated prior to the February 24-March 3 trip by the CPT to Chechnya, which included a visit to Chernokozovo. Then, as more international bodies demanded and received access to Chernokozovo, conditions improved radically; indeed, by April it had become a showcase.

The Russian Commission Visit

During the first week of February, a government commission visited Chernokozovo; it appeared to consist of military staff, but its exact composition and agenda remain unclear.[114] The visitors sought out and found prisoners who had been beaten, even though many inmates had been temporarily transferred out in advance, took special interest in those who had visible signs of injury, and in some cases attempted to document suspected abuse. However, inmates had been forewarned not complain about abuse and those who did were later beaten.

"Salman Sulumov" told Human Rights Watch that before the visit, he was held for three days in a train car, and returned to the facility after the commission left:

---

[113]Human Rights Watch interview with "Alimkhan Visaev," Ingushetia, March 22, 2000.

[114]"Movsar Larsanov" told Human Rights Watch that a man who said he was the head of the prison accompanied the "commission." Human Rights Watch interview, Ingushetia, May 25, 2000. Human Rights Watch wrote to the procurator general to request information about the commission and its agenda. As of this writing we have received no response.

The Chernokozovo Detention Center

When I spent four days at Chernokozovo [approximately February 4], we heard they were expecting some commission. We were [taken] to a train. After [three days], we were brought back to Chernokozovo.... They kept us in the cell one day, then loaded us on the vehicles again where we spent a whole day. Maybe they were hiding us from another commission. Then, we were returned back to the cell.[115]

"Bislan Magomadov," who was present at Chernokozovo for the "commission" visit, emphasized that guards had threatened inmates not to speak candidly about their treatment:

They prepared the cells before the commission came, they made some cots. I don't know what the commission was, but they came from Moscow. They asked how we were fed, whether we go through beatings, what our life was like. But we couldn't complain and could not tell the truth. The guards had told us, "if you complain, we will punish you." We heard that the commission arrived and the same day we were warned that we couldn't complain.[116]

A man who identified himself as the chief of the prison and who accompanied the visitors had been tipped off that an inmate in cell 17, "Aslan Aslanov," had been beaten. While in cell 17, this man examined "Aslanov" and upon the latter's suggestion, examined "Movsar Larsanov" as well. "Larsanov" told Human Rights Watch:

When they examined ["Aslanov"] they saw traces of beatings...At this time, [the Russian leading the delegation] said, "I am the chief of this prison." He made me take off my clothes from the waist up, and asked me if I had been beaten. I said no. But he said, "I am not new to this." He didn't say anything to the guards.[117]

Another detainee, "Ali Baigiraev," had been brutally beaten two days prior to the commission visit. Yet when the commission examined him, at first he denied that he had been beaten, fearing reprisals should he tell the truth:

---

[115]Human Rights Watch interview with "Salman Sulumov" (not his real name), aged forty-six, February 20, 2000.

[116]Human Right Watch interview with "Bislan Magomadov" (not his real name), aged forty-two, February 20, 2000

[117]Human Rights Watch interview with "Movsar Larsanov," Ingushetia, May 25, 2000.

> I first said I just fell down, but then they took us to a private room and made an investigation. They made us tell them about the beatings.... All those who went through severe beatings had to sign a statement [documenting the beatings]. But I think it was just a formality, those responsible will not be punished.[118]

"Baigiraev's" cellmate was brutally beaten in reprisal for telling the commission the cause of his injuries. The commission had examined the young man, who was from the village of Ishcherskaia, because he was visibly bruised. "Umar Khakimov," another cellmate, told Human Rights Watch, "When the commission came he complained. He was bruised, and that is why they questioned him. He was questioned by a general, and the general ordered all those on duty when he was beaten to come and he yelled at them, saying, 'Do you think you will remain unpunished?'"[119]

"Ali Baigiraev" confirmed this account:

> After the commission left, the soldiers learned that [the man from Ishcherskaia] complained and took him out and beat him again. They wanted him to sign a paper with the same confession because the previous one was taken away by the prosecutor. They beat him twice that night.[120]

On February 10, the personnel staffing Chernokozovo were rotated out and Major General Mikhail S. Nazarkin of the Penal Enforcement Department became director of the facility.[121] Most interviewees told Human Rights Watch that abuses lessened after February 10.

International Outrage and Russian Denial

Just before the change in command, details about conditions and unspeakable abuse in the center were leaked to journalists in Ingushetia, allegedly by a guard who had served in Chernokozovo.[122] The second week of

---

[118] Human Rights Watch interview with "Ali Baigiraev," Ingushetia, February 21, 2000
[119] Human Rights Watch interview with "Umar Khakimov," February 21, 2000.
[120] Human Rights Watch interview with "Ali Baigiraev," Ingushetia, February 21, 2000
[121] Maura Reynolds, "Journalists Tour Notorious Chechen Prison," Los Angeles Times Home Edition, February 29, 2000
[122] There had been rumors about the large-scale detention and torture in Chernokozovo as early as January 2000.

February, the guard's letter "to the world" appeared in Ingushetia, dated February 3, which described the beating of Radio Liberty correspondent Andrei Babitsky as well as the torture and rape of other detainees.[123] Around the same time, released detainees began making their way to Ingushetia, and confirmed the extent of the torture.[124]

An international scandal brewed, to which Russian authorities later responded with a chorus of denial. On February 14, presidential press secretary Sergei Yasterzhembsky refuted claims of torture in Chernokozovo; four days later he told reporters that they were "misinforming the public" by reporting the abuses.[125] The Ministry of Justice issued a press release stating that "cases of violence, harassment, torture, and even shootings of persons kept in the investigation ward located in the residential area of Chernokozovo...do not correspond to the [sic] reality and grossly distort the real state of affairs."[126] On March 1, after Andrei Babitsky had been released and made public the treatment to which he was subjected, Minister of Internal Affairs Vladimir Rushailo responded with snide skepticism. "All of [Babitsky's] stories about 250 blows with a baton—I seriously doubt them, as I think we all do."[127]

Meanwhile, the facility underwent further renovation—it was painted, improvements were made in the food rations, and detainees were transferred to other locations to relieve the severe overcrowding in anticipation of expected international delegations. For example, on February 22, "Movsar Larsanov," was transferred to the Chervlyonnaia railway station, where he spent seven days in prisoner transport train carriages, known as "Stolypin Carriages."[128]

---

[123] Andrei Zolotov Jr, "Letter: Babitsky Saw Torture," *Moscow Times*, February 11, 2000. The letter was initially given to a *Le Monde* journalist by a woman who said its author wanted it to be made available to the world. Russian forces arrested Babitsky, detained him at Chernokozovo, and then "exchanged" him to a Chechen field commander.

[124] See Human Rights Watch, "Hundreds of Chechens Detained in 'Filtration Camps': Detainees Face Torture, Extortion, Rape," February 18, 2000.

[125] Patrick Cockburn, "Russia rattled by torture claims at Chechen camps," *Independent*, February 18, 2000.

[126] "Russian Justice Ministry Denies Atrocity Reports," World News Connection, Itar-Tass, February 26, 2000.

[127] "Angry Russia defends its rights record before Washington," Agence France-Presse, March 1, 2000.

[128] In Russian, *Stolipynskie vagony*, named after Tsar Nicolas II's ruthless prime minister, Petr Stolypin, who orchestrated a mass deportation of Chechens at the turn of the century.

They took twenty-four of us by [prisoner transport vehicles], they took us in the morning, that was on the February 22, because on February 21, at night, we were shaved, they made a *prozharka* [i.e. their clothes were sterilized]. In Chervlyonnaia, there were other people there when we arrived. We were in carriages.[129]

Seven days later, "Movsar Larsanov" was returned to Chernokozovo, whereupon other detainees told him that in his absence, another commission had visited Chernokozovo. This commission, most likely the European Committee for the Prevention of Torture (CPT), was comprised of international experts as well as Russians.

In a separate investigation of the cover-up in advance of the CPT visit, Amnesty International also established that "on 25 or 26 February, just a few days before the CPT official visit to Chernokozovo, the Russian authorities reportedly removed about 300 men and women detainees—almost the entire population of Chernokozovo—from the camp to another location in the village of Stanitsa Chervlyonnaya in Chechnya. It is believed that the 300 detainees were removed from the camp by the authorities to hide the real scale of atrocities committed in Chernokozovo."[130]

The CPT was granted permission to visit Chernokozovo during its February 26-March 3 trip to the North Caucasus. In preliminary observations, it expressed satisfaction that at the time of its visit "persons detained in this establishment are not being physically ill-treated."[131] However, the delegation also stated that "many persons detained at Chernokozovo were physically ill-treated in the establishment during the period December 1999 to early February 2000," and described the same methods detailed in this report. The statement explicitly

---

[129]Human Rights Watch interview with "Movsar Larsanov," Ingushetia, February 25, 2000.

[130]Amnesty International press release, "Real Scale of Atrocities in Chechnya: New Evidence of Cover-Up," March 24, 2000.

[131]European Committee for the Prevention of Torture and Inhuman or Degrading Treatment or Punishment Press Release, "Situation in the North Caucasus: Russian authorities release observations by Council of Europe Anti-Torture Committee delegation," April 3, 2000.

requested an investigation by Russian authorities.[132] If the Russian authorities have initiated such an investigation, its results have not been made public.

Russian authorities finally allowed a group of foreign journalists access to Chernokozovo on February 29. The journalists were allowed to talk to a few selected inmates, who denied they had been abused. One of them was "Movsar Larsanov," who later told Human Rights Watch that he had not told the journalists about his transfer to Chervlyonnaya, nor the full extent of the abuses in Chernokozovo, out of fear of retribution from the guards.[133]

Nevertheless, it quickly became clear to the journalists visiting the facility that they were witnessing a cover-up. According to one journalist, who kept away from the guards, the inmates confirmed that the camp "had been transformed in the space of a week in preparation for the arrival of foreign visitors." One detainee muttered to the journalists, "Before that it was like a horror film in here. Everything you hear about this camp is true. They beat people terribly."[134]

On February 17, 2000, then-acting president Vladimir Putin appointed Vladimir Kalamanov as special representative for human rights in Chechnya, amidst the uproar over Chernokozovo as well as international humanitarian law violations in Chechnya. In the wake of visits by the CPT and foreign journalists, and less than two weeks into his job, Kalamanov claimed that there had been no torture in Chernokozovo; he continued to categorically deny the allegations on other occasions.[135] To his credit, by July Kalamanov's mission in Znamenskoye

---

[132]Specifically, the CPT stated the following: "[I]t is of crucial importance, in the interests of the prevention of ill-treatment, for what happened in the establishment during the period December 1999 to early February 2000 to be the subject of a thorough and independent inquiry and for appropriate sanctions to be imposed on those responsible for ill-treatment. In application of Article 8, paragraph 5 of the Convention [European Convention for the Prevention of Torture and Inhuman or Degrading Treatment or Punishment], the delegation requests that such an inquiry be carried out without delay and that the Russian authorities inform the CPT of its outcome within three months. Further, the delegation calls upon the Russian authorities to remain particularly vigilant with regard to the manner in which prisoners are treated at Chernokozovo." Ibid.

[133]Human Rights Watch with "Movsar Larsanov," Ingushetia, May 25, 2000.

[134]Amelia Gentleman, "Fresh Paint Fails to Hide Stench of Fear," *Guardian*, March 2, 2000; Patrick E. Tyler, "At Russian Camp, Two Views of Chechen Prisoners," *New York Times*, March 1, 2000.

[135]He said, "It is a glaring lie to portray Chernokozovo as a place where people are shot and tortured almost every day." "Kalamanov says no filtration camps in Chechnya," Itar-Tass, March 1, 2000. Later that month, he said, "None of the delegations have confirmed rumors of torture or humiliation.... In each case when torture is in question, I must be

had helped to secure the release and amnesty of more than 200 inmates at Chernokozovo and other detention centers.[136]

---

contacted because I am responsible for the observation of human rights in Chechnya... We have not received such information...." "Human rights commissioner denies Chechnya torture reports," Interfax News Agency, March 29, 2000.

[136]Council of Europe press release, "Council of Europe mission continues to make significant progress in Chechnya," July 21, 2000.

ABUSES AND TORTURE IN OTHER PLACES OF DETENTION

Other detention facilities for Chechen detainees have included remand prisons in Russia proper; makeshift facilities at a dormitory and a factory in Chechnya; and ad-hoc holding facilities—earthen pits or metal storage containers—on Russian military bases in Chechnya and in Russia proper. Detainees were frequently transferred among facilities, and many Human Rights Watch interviewees who provided testimony about Chernokozovo also described other facilities to which they were transferred. Identifying the legal status of the latter detention locations is difficult, while the legal grounds for arrests have never been established. Most detainees were not told the status of any charges against them during their detention, nor were most given any written acknowledgment of their detention upon their release. [137]

---

[137] A sampling of detention centers and their legal status is available by examining the list of centers visited by the CPT. SIZOs [Sledstvennyi izoliator, or pre-trial detention centers] are under the jurisdiction of the Ministry of Justice, IVSs [Izoliator vremennogo soderzhaniia, or temporary holding cells at police facilities] are under the jurisdiction of the Interior Ministry. Both hold pre-trial detainees.

On its first visit, from February 27 to March 4, 2000, the CPT visited the following facilities: SIZO No. 1, Grozny; SIZO No. 2, Chernokozovo; IVS, Chervlyonnaya Station; IVS, Naurskiy District Department of Internal Affairs; IVS, Shali District Department of Internal Affairs; IVS, Temporary Internal Affairs Department of Grozny Selsky District (Tolstoy Yurt); the former holding facility, Goryacheistochnenskoye (Tolstoy Yurt); SIZO No. 1, Vladikavkaz (North Ossetia); IVS, Mozdok District Department of Internal Affairs (North Ossetia); and SIZO No. 2, Pyatigorsk (Stavropol). The delegation also went to hospitals in Naurskiy and Tolstoy Yurt and spoke with members of the local population in several of the localities visited, including Grozny. CPT Press Release, "Visit by the European Committee for the Prevention of Torture to the North Caucasian region of the Russian Federation," March 6, 2000.

On its second visit, from April 20 to 27, 2000, the CPT visited the following facilities: SIZO No. 2, Chernokozovo; Oktyabrskiy District Temporary Department of Internal Affairs, Grozny; Zavodskoy District Temporary Department of Internal Affairs, Grozny; Temporary Department of Internal Affairs, Gudermes; Unit of the Federal Security Service, Khankala Base of the Allied Group of Armed Forces; Unit of the Ministry of Internal Affairs, Khankala Base of the Allied Group of Armed Forces; Temporary Department of Internal Affairs, Shelkovskaya; Temporary Department of Internal Affairs, Urus-Martan; Regional Department of Internal Affairs, Urus-Martan; Department of the Federal Security Service, Urus-Martan; SIZO of the Federal Security Service in North Ossetia-Alania, Vladikavkaz (North Ossetia); Territory Hospital at Colony No. 3, Georgievsk (Stavropol Territory); and

Stavropol territory

Five Chernokozovo detainees interviewed by Human Rights Watch were eventually transferred to remand prisons in the cities of Stavropol or Pyatigorsk, both in the Stavropol province of the Russian Federation.

Former inmates at the Pyatigorsk facility, nicknamed "Belyi Lebed"—"White Swan"— said that, like at Chernokozovo, upon arrival they were met by a gauntlet of soldiers who beat them. The facility is most likely SIZO No.2. "Issa Habuliev" described his arrival on February 18 from Chernokozovo:

> We were taken during the day [from Chernokozovo] and by the evening we were there. There was a corridor, on two sides there were soldiers the whole way, we were beaten from each side, with batons.... There were twenty-four [detainees] with me, including three women.[138]

None of those interviewed by Human Rights Watch were interrogated in Pyatigorsk, and none said that they were beaten after the initial "welcome gauntlet."

On February 22, many of the former Chernokozovo inmates were transferred from Pyatigorsk to the Stavropol Central Prison, apparently in preparation for a commission visit to "Belyi Lebed." Issa Habuliev told Human Rights Watch: "When the commission was going to come, all the prisoners were mixed together. Of the twenty-four who had been with me [when brought to Pyatigorsk], five wounded and one woman were kept behind, the others were taken to Stavropol."[139] In Stavropol, the detainees were again beaten, gauntlet-style, when they arrived, and throughout the intake process. As in Pyatigorsk, after this process they were not beaten. "Magomed Kantiev" sarcastically described the welcome at the Stavropol prison: "They accepted us very warmly. As a result, I only was able to get up on the fourth day, and after eleven or twelve days, I could finally walk again. They beat all of us, it was the time of the February 23 holidays [Red Army Day, popularly celebrated as "International Man's Day"] and they were drunk."[140]

During the intake inspection, guards examined detainees' bodies for bruises and other marks left by handling weapons, and forced the men to do exercises,

---

SIZO No. 2, Pyatigorsk (Stavropol Territory). CPT Press Release, "Second visit to the North Caucasus by the European Anti-Torture Committee" May 2, 2000.

[138]Human Rights Watch interview with "Issa Habuliev," Ingushetia, April 8, 2000.
[139]Ibid.
[140]Human Rights Watch interview with "Magomed Kantiev," May 13, 2000.

Abuses and Torture in Other Places of Detention

beating them during the process. "Magomed Kantiev" described this to Human Rights Watch:

> They made us take off our clothes and checked us completely, all over the body, very thoroughly. While this was taking place, they made us do...deep-knee bends, and during these exercises they beat us with clubs. After these beatings, we were led to the bathroom, in groups of three or four. We went down a hall on the first floor and up to the second floor, and there again there was a "live corridor" [gauntlet] which led to the bathroom.[141]

"Aslanbek Digaev" and "Issa Habuliev," who also said that they were severely beaten when they were admitted to Stavropol, reported that the worst beatings took place in the bathroom, where they were again forced to do deep-knee bends. "Digaev" gave the following account:

> In the bath they took off all our clothes and said they had to warm them [to have them sterilized]. We gave them our clothes.... They had some rubber clubs, new ones. If you got a blow, it stuck to your body, you couldn't see the effect immediately, only after the second or third day, then there were black stripes. At this time we were beaten very violently, until death's door.[142]

"Magomed Kantiev" confirmed this:

> There were seven or eight men standing and they had clubs, some in both hands, and we were beaten so badly there that we eventually all fell to the ground....We had our arms around each others' shoulders, and they made us continue [doing the knee bend exercises] until we fell. As soon as you stopped, the guards beat us with clubs, on our bare skin. Those who couldn't stand, there was one who fell, they dragged him aside and beat him again. At the end, all of us were laying there, exhausted. All eighty or ninety of us had to do this, for them it made no difference if you were weak or strong, and so when it finally came time to go into the bath, no one could walk, we all had to crawl. And during

---

[141]Human Rights Watch interview with "Magomed Kantiev," Ingushetia, May 13, 2000.
[142]Human Rights Watch interview with "Aslanbek Digaev," Ingushetia, May 16, 2000.

this time they beat us, until all eighty or ninety had gone through. Then we had to go to our cells, again through the "live corridor."[143]

Military bases

Mozdok

During the first Chechnya war, the Russian military base at Mozdok, North Ossetia, became notorious for the torture of Chechen detainees held there. In 1999 and 2000, numerous internally displaced persons anxious about the fate of missing relatives feared that they had been detained at Mozdok, and Russian officials at checkpoints and border crossings often threatened to send Chechen males there. Human Rights Watch found at least three cases of severe beatings to the male genitalia of prisoners at one, and perhaps more, facilities in Mozdok.

"Idris Batukaev" was detained at a checkpoint outside Grozny and held in Mozdok from December 19, 1999 until March 3, 2000. He told Human Rights Watch that he was held in the basement of the prison facility, in a cell that he shared with several others. The cells had concrete floors and slabs of wood for beds.

He was ill-treated when there was a shift change, when taken for questioning, during questioning, and also when he asked to use the toilet. Sometimes guards did not permit him to go to the toilet. "If you could know, in reality, what a disgrace it was. You can go crazy. They humiliated men."[144]

On one night in February, the guards brought a detainee to "Idris Batukaev's" cell and sodomized him with batons:

> He was brought at night, the only thing I managed to ask was where he was from. They didn't even take off his handcuffs.... Then they came into the cell, beat him, and did those other things.... They came, they beat him with rifle butts, then came with dogs, you couldn't avoid

---

[143] Human Rights Watch interview with "Magomed Kantiev," Ingushetia, May 13, 2000. Memorial also shared with Human Rights Watch the details of an interview with a former Chernokozovo detainee who had been transferred to Pyatigorsk and Stavropol at the end of February. The man reported being forced to do identical exercises in the bathroom described by "Magomed Kantiev." Human Rights Watch interview with researcher for Memorial, May 6, 2000.

[144] Human Rights Watch interview with "Idris Batukaev," aged twenty-seven, Ingushetia, April 26, 2000.

Abuses and Torture in Other Places of Detention

them.... They were raping him, with clubs.... They took the [victim] away immediately afterwards.[145]

"Idris Batukaev" himself was interrogated on numerous occasions during his detention. He described having to walk up two flights from the basement, blindfolded, and then through the gauntlet each time:

> They put a sack on my head, and I had to pass through a corridor, I was beaten with clubs, until I got to their room. I was taken several times, they were FSB or GRU.[146] They asked me if I had taken part in the war, they wanted me to sign something, they tortured me, asking questions...you put your hands on the table, and they beat you with clubs or batons. They kicked me, with their boots on. They beat me with batons on the legs as well, I was standing, with my legs spread.[147]

"Idris Batukaev" was also severely beaten to his genitals; he alluded to the loss of a testicle as a result of these beatings. "They tortured me. I can't walk, it is difficult for me to go to the toilet. They beat me, in men's places...they beat it off, with clubs."[148] When interviewed more than six weeks after his release, "Idris Batukaev" still clearly had difficulty walking, and reported that he suffered from severe pains in his chest and abdomen. Human Rights Watch spoke to "Idris Batukaev's" wife, who said that her husband's genitals were swollen, that he frequently had blood in his urine and suffered from constipation and impotence, saying "As a man, he's useless."[149] He had only begun to seek medical treatment, because traveling to Ingushetia brought on the fear of being rearrested.

Human Rights Watch interviewed a woman whose husband was detained for approximately one month in Mozdok and had to be hospitalized after his release in early April 2000. She told Human Rights Watch that her husband also had been beaten severely in his genitals.[150] In addition, a surgeon at an Ingushetia hospital treated a seventeen- or eighteen-year-old boy who had been detained in

---

[145]Ibid.
[146]Glavnoe Razvedevatelnoye Upravlenie, or military intelligence.
[147]Human Rights Watch interview with "Idris Batukaev," Ingushetia, April 26, 2000.
[148]Ibid.
[149]Human Rights Watch interview with "Idris Batukaev's" wife, Ingushetia, April 26, 2000.
[150]Human Rights Watch interview with "Zina Salmanova" (not her real name), age unknown, Ingushetia, April 18, 2000.

Mozdok and said he had been beaten in the genitals. The surgeon reported that the boy's genitals were swollen and that there were indications he may have been sodomized, as he had suffered internal injuries to his colon. Despite the need for medical intervention, the young man refused to be hospitalized for fear that he might be rearrested while receiving treatment. The surgeon said that between twenty and thirty former detainees had sought medical treatment for injuries resulting from beatings and torture, and that many said they had been detained at Mozdok.[151]

"Idris Batukaev" reported that towards the end of his detention, improvements were made to the upper floors of the detention center, but not to his cell block. He believed that the prison authorities preparing for a visiting delegation—possibly the CPT—which visited the Mozdok detention facility in late February.[152]

Khankala

Russian forces captured the military base at Khankala, a large complex spanning several kilometers, on December 12, 1999. Human Rights Watch interviewed eight people who were detained there in January and February 2000, and has additional information about other detainees from relatives and research shared by Memorial. The CPT visited Khankala on its second visit to the North Caucasus in April 2000; although it has not publicly described the nature of facilities used for such purposes, it reports that as of at least April 27, detainees continued to be held there.[153] Human Rights Watch received many reports of severe beatings at Khankala, and one report of rape.

None of the detainees held at Khankala were kept in even minimally acceptable facilities. According to three Human Rights Watch interviewees, prisoners at Khankala in late January and early February were kept for days in parked, overcrowded prisoner transport vehicles, usually meant to hold detainees for several hours at most.[154] They were given little or nothing to eat and no sanitary facilities. The vehicles remained outside, in the bitter cold, and were unheated. Women were also held in cages outside the vehicles, including

---

[151] Human Rights Watch interview with doctor speaking on condition of anonymity, Ingushetia, March 25, 2000.

[152] Human Rights Watch interview with "Idris Batukaev," Ingushetia, April 26, 2000.

[153] Detainees were in the custody, apparently of the Ministry of Internal Affairs or the FSB.

[154] These are "Magomed Kantiev," "Salman Sulumov," and Andrei Babitsky. In colloquial Russian, this vehicle may be called GAZ 53, *avtozak*, or *voronok*. It is a truck, with two compartments in the trailer that serve as holding cells.

Abuses and Torture in Other Places of Detention

"Fatimah Akhmedova," who at the time was six months pregnant and who told Human Rights Watch of three other women kept in cages. "Akhmedova," who arrived at Khankala on January 28, described the cages:

> The cage was small, there was a bench. We couldn't raise our heads. The cage was outside on the ground, like a cage for tigers [at a zoo] and it was snowing. I was given one plastic bottle with ice which I used [as drinking water] for two days. I was given no food, and was not let out to use the toilet.[155]

At least one female was raped at Khankala. "Akhmedova" described her as a fourteen-year-old girl, but after learning her full identity from other sources, Human Rights Watch ascertained that she was nineteen. According to "Akhmedova," the young woman shared a cage with her intermittently, and told her she had been raped:

> She was detained before I arrived at Khankala.... This girl, [gives name], was brought to me for five or ten minutes at a time. She was brought and taken out three times at night. She was kept in a tent, for three days, while they raped her, and ripped her clothes. Then she was dressed in military clothes and taken to Chernokozovo on January 31. She herself said she was raped, and I saw the lower part of her body [her genital region] covered in blood.... She was always kept in the tent, but I sometimes heard her screaming. They brought her the first time on January 29, and took her out three times. I met her again in Chernokozovo later.[156]

The Russian human rights organization Memorial, with the assistance of Human Rights Watch, located the girl at her parents' house in Chechnya. Her sisters told Memorial that she had been arrested on January 24 and was detained for eighteen days, but did not know where. The Memorial researcher saw, but did not interview, the traumatized young woman, who suffers from epilepsy and may be mentally ill.[157]

---

[155] Human Rights Watch interview with "Fatimah Akhmedova," Ingushetia, March 7, 2000.
[156] Ibid.
[157] Human Rights Watch interview with Memorial researcher, Nazran, Ingushetia, May 15, 2000. The victim apparently looks far younger than her nineteen years.

Guards severely beat male inmates on the way into the prisoner-transport vehicles, inside the vehicles, on the way to interrogations, and during interrogations.

"Movsar Larsanov," who had been arrested on January 15 at the Staraia Sunzha checkpoint outside Grozny, was transferred to Khankala with three other men; all were beaten severely as they were loaded onto the prisoner-transport vehicle:

> They put sacks on our heads. We were sitting on the ground, I saw sacks in their hands, then they put it over my head and tied it. I had my hands behind my head, they grabbed me by the collar and said "be quick," but it was difficult. I heard them beat another one of the guys.... He lost a tooth because of that. They beat me too, on the back of my head and on the face, and then across my fingers [indicates across knuckles of the right hand]. They kicked me. They beat all of us. Then we were put in a prisoner transport vehicle.[158]

"Badrudi Kantaev" was held in Khankala only one day after his arrest in the Chernorechiye district of Grozny on February 5, but by the end of May he still had small scars under both his eyes, which he said were caused by a blow from a rifle butt.

> They beat me terribly.... They would just punch you, and say, "You damn Chechen, why aren't you falling over!" and then once they had beaten you enough to fall down, they would say, "Why did you fall down, get up." I was on my feet, and then they punched me, and when I fell, they then hit me with a rifle butt, in the face.[159]

Interrogations took place in tents not far from the prisoner-transport vehicles. "Salman Sulumov," held in Khankala from January 28 to 31, was beaten before he was ever asked a question.

> I was taken to interrogation and shown into a tent.... When I entered I was told to go up to the table with my hands behind my neck. I obeyed, thinking they would just examine me ...then I felt a kick [from behind] in my kidney. When I asked why they did this, they said I must not ask

---

[158]Human Rights Watch interview with "Movsar Larsanov," Ingushetia, May 25, 2000.

[159]Human Rights Watch interview with "Badrudi Kantaev" (not his real name), aged forty-nine, Ingushetia, May 26, 2000.

any questions. They said that was only the beginning, that they would smash my head with the guns. There were four of them in the room, they were all armed with guns. They were not conscript soldiers, they were either OMON or *kontraktniki*.[160]

I said to the soldiers that if I had some information to give I would give it, but that they didn't need to beat me. They agreed.[161]

"Sultan Deniev," who was arrested in Gekhi Chu on February 7 and detained at Khankala until approximately February 11, described being tortured with a soldering iron during interrogation. He showed Human Rights Watch a small scar, which he said was from the burns he received. On February 10, guards took Deniev from the prisoner transport vehicle to the interrogation tent:

[They made me] pull my sweater over my head so all I could see was his boots, I couldn't see his face. For ten minutes they beat me and took me into some kind of tent. They stripped me to the waist and beat me again. They slapped me with a [handgun] and used the soldering iron. They burnt me on the hands, back and legs.[162]

An expatriate researcher who travelled to Gekhi Chu in April 2000 spoke to a man there who had been detained at the same time as "Sultan Deniev." His account corroborated that of "Sultan Deniev," including reports that men had been burned with soldering irons while detained in Khankala.[163]

Although all former detainees interviewed by Human Rights Watch had been held there in late January or early February, information from other sources suggests that detainees were tortured for months thereafter. "Askerkhan Umarkhanov," a journalist, told Human Rights Watch that he accompanied staff of the Russian Emergency Situations Ministry (MChS) on a visit to what appeared to be a checkpoint within the Khankala military base on April 5. There,

---

[160] Contract soldiers work on short-term military service contracts. Chechen civilians usually describe Russian soldiers as being either *srochniki*—conscripts—or *kontraktniki*—contract soldiers. Conscript soldiers are usually identifiable by their young age. Chechen civilians typically use the blanket term "kontraktniki" for all other Russian forces.

[161] Human Rights Watch interview with "Salman Sulumov," Ingushetia, February 20, 2000.

[162] Human Rights Watch interview with "Sultan Deniev," Ingushetia, April 18, 2000.

[163] The researcher has requested anonymity. Nazran, Ingushetia, April 22, 2000.

he viewed the corpses of two men that bore signs of torture, and saw men being beaten there.

According to "Umarkhanov," MChS had received a call on April 3, were told that there were six men in detention at Khankala, and MChS should come "in a few days." On April 5, the MChS workers, accompanied by guards, collected two bodies from Khankala:

> It was clear that they had been beaten. One had a broken arm, it was in a wooden splint. They had been shot in the legs, both had black and blue heels, from beating.... We wrote down a description of the bodies, the color of the eyes, teeth, and so on, so the relatives could identify them. They had been beaten very badly, when we lifted them, the spine [of one] was broken, the body was flexible in strange places, not stiff like you would expect a corpse to be.... We searched their pockets, behind their ears, everywhere, to find notes or anything to document who they were. But there was nothing.[164]

According to "Askerkhan Umarkhanov" the bodies of the victims were buried, unidentified, by MChS in Alkhan-Kala, a village on the western outskirts of Grozny.

Other Military Encampments

Human Rights Watch received reports of detainees being tortured at other military encampments. Saipudin Saadulayev, aged thirty-nine, was a witness to several killings in the Staropromyslovski district of Grozny, documented in an earlier Human Rights Watch report.[165] On January 22 or 23, soldiers brought him and seven other detainees to a military camp in the Karpinsky district, near the Russian Orthodox cemetery, and put them in a deep pit.[166] Human Rights Watch independently located one of the other seven men, "Aslanbek Digaev," who described it as a place known locally as Solyonaia Balka; both men

---

[164] Human Rights Watch interview with "Askerkhan Umarkhanov" (not his real name), age unknown, Ingushetia, April 24, 2000.

[165] "Civilian Killings in the Staropromyslovski District of Grozny," *A Human Rights Watch Short Report*, vol. 12, no. 2(D), February 2000. The testimony of Saadulayev can be found on pages 10 and 11 of that report.

[166] This incident happened soon after a Russian general had been killed by Chechen fighters. Although Saipudin Saadulayev reports the date as January 22, "Aslanbek Digaev" and relatives of the other Karpinky detainees said the men were arrested on January 23.

described the soldiers stationed there as from different regions and noted that at least some of them were OMON troops.

Shortly after they were put in the pit, a soldier entered the pit and began beating them, saying, "You dogs, you sheep, you were killing our comrades. Now we will show you!" OMON troops were watching from the top of the pit, laughing. After the beating, the soldiers ordered the men to remove their hats and poured water on them. "It was cold and I was wet all over, and the water began to freeze," said Saipudin Saadulayev.

According to "Aslanbek Digaev," the soldiers also threw heavy objects onto the detainees in the trench. "They picked up big stones and dropped them into the trench, they struck us. The trenches were four meters deep, it was around the camp. They threw big stones, one hit me on the head."[167]

The next day, the eight men were loaded onto a truck, handcuffed painfully to the railing. They were taken to another military camp between Grozny and Argun where they were detained in a wire cage on the back of a prisoner transport vehicle together with nine other men. The men were briefly questioned by a Russian official before being put back on the truck: "It was very cold in the truck, even worse than in the pit. Our boots were wet. We had to stand up [because it was so crowded], but the roof was too low to stand straight."[168] At 2:00 a.m., a group of soldiers came and beat some of the men, punching them and using rubber batons, taking two men's leather coats before leaving: "The whole night we had to warm each other, sharing one jacket," Saipudin Saadulaev said. The next day, Saadulaev managed to secure his release by promising to return to Grozny to try to help find a missing Russian soldier. Four of the eighteen men were released together with Saipudin Saadulaev. "Digaev" and the other six men from Karpinky were then transferred to Chernokozovo.

Soldiers routinely detain and abuse civilians at military positions. "Khamzat Vakuev" was taken to a field between Serzhen Yurt and Shali after he was detained on April 28, in the wake of an attack on a convoy in the area.[169] He and four other detainees were kept in the field overnight, handcuffed and with their feet tied together with wire.

> They beat us very often. As soon as they drank, they would beat us. They humiliated us.... They would put their fingers right to our noses, and flick it. There was no interrogation. They just asked questions, they

---

[167]Human Rights Watch interview with "Aslanbek Digaev," Ingushetia, May 16, 2000.
[168]Human Rights Watch interview with Saipudin Saadulaev, Ingushetia, February 4, 2000.
[169]Human Rights Watch interview with "Khamzat Vakuev," May 26, 2000.

wanted me to confess to taking part in the attack on the convoy, but they knew I wasn't a fighter.... At the field there were only soldiers, no other prisoners. They have pits there, but they didn't put me in a pit. There were so many soldiers there that they didn't need to guard us. I tried not to move around, I was trying to stay with the ones who had already beaten me, so I wouldn't be beaten again.[170]

The following day "Khamzat Vakuev" was separated from the other men, put in a truck, and taken to another military encampment near Ersenoi, where he was put in a trench. "Everywhere there were trenches. They put me in a trench in Ersenoi.... In Ersenoi I was not beaten very violently, just a little bit. When I was in the trench, then passing soldiers can kick you or slap you, as they like."[171] When Human Rights Watch interviewed "Vakuev," he was seeking medical treatment in Ingushetia; he had been hospitalized following his release because he was coughing blood, he was also diagnosed with prolapsed kidneys, a condition associated with the effects of severe beatings.[172]

Six men detained in Tsotsin Yurt on April 27 were also held in a covered pit for five days. Two of the men were removed from the facility on May 2, and were left by the side of the road, severely injured from the ill-treatment and harsh conditions in which they had been held. One, Zhebir Turpalkhanov, died a half hour after he arrived home. Although no autopsy was performed, his relatives believe the beatings and harsh conditions in detention were a contributing factor, if not the cause, of his death.[173] The other, Akhmed Abuyev, who survived, believed that the pair had been left for dead. He was interviewed by the local head of administration on a videotape prepared by villagers, in which he said that he was severely beaten with truncheons, and stabbed with a large skewer typically used in the region for shish-kebab. On the videotape, Akhmed Abuyev shows parts of his body where he was injured: clearly visible are stab-like wounds near his right shoulder and on both shins, and a wound that appeared to be an abrasion on the left shin. In addition, his right upper arm appeared bruised. Zhebir Turpalkhanov's body is also shown on the videotape; although the body was covered with a sheet, what appeared to be bruising was visible on

---

[170]Ibid.
[171]Ibid.
[172]Ibid.
[173]Human Rights Watch interview with Tahir Turpalkhanov, aged thirty-seven, Nazran, Ingushetia, May 15, 2000. Tahir Turpalkhanov's account of events was supported by a video made by a resident of Tsotsin Yurt, who filmed some of the alleged vandalism, interviewed several witnesses as well as a released detainee.

his left collarbone.[174] According to a relative, before he died Zhebir Turpalkhanov said that although blindfolded, he believed the pit where they were held was in a military encampment because he frequently heard helicopters taking off and landing.[175]

Other Ad-hoc Detention Centers

Tolstoy Yurt

At least one building of the "NGD" oil refinery outside Tolstoy Yurt was used as a detention center from at least early February until February 16. Former detainees described the facility as a "basement" or a "half earthen" structure, with one large room where all the detainees were held. Upon release, one detainee was given a certificate that indicated that the facility was under the authority of the Ministry of Justice, at least during the time of his detention from February 7 to 16.[176] However, at that time the Ministry of Justice claimed that Chernokozovo was the only detention facility in Chechnya under its authority.[177]

"Sultan Deniev," who had initially been arrested in Gekhi Chu on February 7, was transferred to Tolstoy Yurt or around February 11. He told Human Rights Watch that during interrogation there, he and another man, a boxer who had also been transferred from Khankala, were beaten and threatened with summary execution:

> It was a big building, half-earth, and we saw gas stoves and beds and a crowd of people. There were fifty from Shaami Yurt there, and ten or more from different parts and then twenty or maybe more of us. So in total eighty. It was clean with gas stoves and beds, and I thought that they would be more humane [than at Khankala].[178]

---

[174]Home videotape filmed by a villager from Tsotsin Yurt on May 1 and 2, 2000, given to Human Rights Watch on May 15, 2000 by Tahir Turpalkhanov.

[175]Human Rights Watch interview with Tahir Turpalkhanov, Nazran, Ingushetia, May 15, 2000.

[176]"Sultan Deniev" allowed Human Rights Watch to photograph this certificate.

[177]Deputy Minister of Justice Kalinin was cited on February 7, 2000 as saying "the only detention center in Chechnya which operates at present is located in the settlement of Chernokozovo in the Naursky region." Vladimir Nuyakshev and Yevgeniy Sobetskiy, "Chechnya: Punishment Administering Bodies Restored," Itar-Tass/World News Connection, February 7, 2000.

[178]Human Rights Watch interview with "Sultan Deniev," Ingushetia, April 18, 2000.

> The first day nothing happened, the second day we were fingerprinted and photographed, again [there was] interrogation.... They took a Makarov gun and beat me several times. He was close to breaking my hand, he was twisting it so hard. Me and this boxer [were taken to be interrogated at the same time]. [Afterwards,] the boxer was difficult to recognize, he was red all over and it was difficult for him to stand up, he was beaten so badly....
>
> Then they put me on a wall, and said, "In the name of the Russian Federation, according to Article 208 you will be shot." This was in the second interrogation. I said, "OK, my life is in your hands." I just knew nothing would help. Then they got more angry and said, "What, don't you want to live, are you a fanatic?"[179]

After being threatened with execution, "Sultan Deniev" was returned to the room with the barracks. He was released on February 16.[180]

Tolstoy Yurt held both fighters and civilians. Among the latter were medical professionals (including the Chechen minister of health) who had left Grozny during the general evacuation of the capital by Chechen fighters in early February.[181] A forty-four-year-old pediatrician sustained broken ribs as a result of the beatings at Tolstoy Yurt. Although he cannot travel outside Chechnya because his documents were not returned to him when he was released, Human Rights Watch was able to interview his sister, to whom he had spoken at great length about his detention. She told Human Rights Watch that after he was detained in Grozny, Russian soldiers told him he would be sent to the Urus-Martan hospital, together with the wounded. Instead, however,

> They passed Urus-Martan and went to Tolstoy Yurt, and it was at that point that [my brother] realized that they were being taken to prison, not the hospital. There were many [Russian] generals there, and also [Russian] journalists. They were thrown out of the bus and beaten. At that time, two of [my brother's] ribs were broken. It was very damp and they spent the night there, this was in a sort of basement; 110

---

[179] Ibid.
[180] Ibid.
[181] After being held in Tolstoy Yurt for several days they were transferred to Chernokozovo.

people were counted, and four died during the night. There were twenty physicians, the rest were civilians from the hospital.[182]

"Leyla Saigatova's" husband was the driver of a bus transporting the wounded and the medical personnel. She said her husband had also been held for a similar time in Tolstoy Yurt.[183] Human Rights Watch saw and briefly spoke with the father of a twenty-one-year-old man who had been among the fighters as they left Alkhan-Kala, he also said he was held for a week in Tolstoy Yurt before being transfered to Chernokozovo and then to other detention centers.[184]

The Internat in Urus-Martan[185]

A former boarding school for girls is one of three acknowledged detention centers in the Urus-Martan district.[186] During the interwar period the school served as a religious educational center; it was adapted for use as a detention facility after Russian forces assumed control of Urus-Martan, from at least January 2000. According to three former internat detainees interviewed by Human Rights Watch, the Penza OMON had immediate command responsibility of the facility in January and February, when the abuses we document were committed. The multi-story building is surrounded by a fence with signs indicating that the area is mined.[187] The internat became notorious early on for its filthy conditions and for the abuse of detainees held and interrogated there; the physical conditions improved somewhat after March 2000, but abuse persisted. Amnesty International interviewed two released detainees who were tortured in the internat; one man was brutally gang-raped.[188] During her April visit to Chechnya, U.N. High Commissioner for Human Rights Mary Robinson sought and was denied access to the facility.

---

[182]Human Rights Watch interview with "Roza Yandieva" (not her real name), aged twenty-eight, Ingushetia, 22 April, 2000.

[183]Human Rights Watch interview with "Leyla Saigatova," Ingushetia, April 12, 2000.

[184]Human Rights Watch interview, May 6, 2000.

[185]*Internat* is the Russian term for an orphanage or boarding school.

[186] Detainees in Urus-Martan are also held at the district police station, and at the local FSB department. See, "Second visit to the North Caucasus by the European Anti-Torture Committee," CPT press release, May 2, 2000. Available at www.cpt.coe.int.

[187]Human Rights Watch telephone interview with *Le Monde* journalist Natalie Nougayrede, May 31, 2000.

[188]Amnesty International press release, "Russian Federation: Continuing torture and rape in Chechnya," 8 June 2000.

"Issa Zagoyev," in Urus-Martan, reported that he was held by the "Penza OMON" from January 20-26, 2000. He said there was no heat and no place to sleep:

> For six days, they let me go to the toilet only one time, it was the same for the others. We were thirteen people in a small cell, three by five meters.... It was impossible to stand still because of the cold, I had to jump and run to keep warm. We couldn't sleep because there was only the concrete floor. There was a wooden bench, but it was impossible to sleep. Relatives were allowed to bring food, but the Russians would keep all the food for themselves.[189]

"Issa Zagoyev" was not beaten while at the facility, although he saw other men be beaten.

> They take you out one by one, make you spread your legs and punch you in the eye. A big guy stands there, and they surround you with automatics while the big one beats you, while you are handcuffed. I was not beaten, but I saw the others being beaten...They would beat them and make them lie on the [cold] concrete for hours...[190]

"Abu Uruskhanov" was detained at the internat from February 29 to March 4, 2000, with twenty-eight men in a cell measuring only approximately 2.5 by four or five meters.[191] As soon as he arrived, "Urshukhanov" had to "run the gauntlet" of beatings:

> When we were transferred, there were several [prisoner transport vehicles] full. They opened the door and someone said, "Get out." There was a corridor [gauntlet], and OMON were lining both sides. When you passed through this corridor, you got beaten some with clubs, some kicked us. There were about seventy of us. When I passed, they said, "run," because if you didn't move fast you just got beaten more. So we ran into the internat. There was a big hall, they put us on our knees, with our hands behind our heads facing the wall. We

---

[189]Human Rights Watch interview with "Issa Zagoyev" (not his real name), aged twenty-three, Ingushetia, April 8, 2000.
[190]Ibid.
[191]Human Rights Watch interview with "Abu Uruskhanov" (not his real name), aged thirty, Ingushetia, April 26, 2000.

had to stay that way for more than an hour. But if you got tired, you could lie down on your stomach, if you didn't have the strength to kneel. But the floor was concrete—it was winter, and very cold.[192]

"Abu Uruskhankov" was beaten several times with a club during his first interrogation, and was threatened with torture on another occasion. He told Human Rights Watch that several others detained with him had been severely injured because of beatings.

"Ilyas Makhmadov" was detained at the internat from April 5 to 15, 2000. He described the conditions as significantly less crowded—the number of people in his cell fluctuated between six and ten. He also described the cell as being lice-infested, with plank beds and a bucket in the corner to use as a toilet; there were no bathing facilities.

"Ilyas Makhmadov" was beaten during his first interrogation in an office at the internat, and subsequently threatened. On one occasion, he was forced to sit at a table with his hands clasped behind his neck for approximately two hours, and was beaten with rubber truncheons on the back of his neck and on the top of his hands. After that questioning began. "They were masked, two of them, in police uniform. The same ones questioned me as had beaten me. I could recognize them by their voices. They thought I would never guess who they were, but on other days, they walked around without masks."[193] "Makhmadov" was also beaten by guards in his cell:

> The first two days, the SOBR[194] and OMON had fun with us. They would open the cell, and two or three of them would come in. They would line us up and have some kind of contest, whoever hit the hardest was the winner. If they hit us and we fell down, they would applaud. The other prisoners in my cell told me that before I came this happened every day, but when I got there, this happened only for [a period of] four or five days.[195]

On another occasion, "Makhmadov" was beaten while standing against a wall. "They forced me to lean against it, with my hands on the wall above my

---

[192]Human Rights Watch interview with "Issa Zagoyev," Ingushetia, April 8, 2000.
[193]Human Rights Watch interview with "Ilyas Makhmadov" (not his real name), aged thirty-one, Ingushetia, May 13, 2000.
[194]Spetsialnyi otriad bystrogo otreagirovanii, or rapid reaction forces.
[195]Human Rights Watch interview with "Ilyas Makhmadov," Ingushetia, May 13, 2000.

head. And they kicked me and punched me that way. They would do this during the first two or three days, then they left me alone."[196] As a result of the beatings, for a week afterwards the back of "Makhmadov's" neck was swollen, and he was unable even to turn his head. He also had pain and bruising on his kidneys.

After relatives of seventeen-year-old Said Visaev saw him taken away, they went to the internat on February 10 to see whether he was detained there and to try to bribe officials to release him. A woman approached the relatives and gave them a tip that the body of a boy had been found in the boiler room of the Urus-Martan hospital. There, the relatives found the body of Said Visaev.

> The face was unrecognizable—we identified him by his eyebrows and socks. His mouth was swollen, his right eye was swollen, his left eye was missing and the back of his head was smashed. His hands were bloodied. The boy's uncle said there was a big hole in the back of his head—he suspects it was bashed in by a bayonet. I saw bruises on his chest, large bruises.[197]

Human Rights Watch was unable to confirm whether Said Visaev suffered these lethal wounds in the internat or in another facility in Urus-Martan.

When the U.N. High Commissioner for Human Rights, Mary Robinson, visited Chechnya on April 3, 2000, she requested, but was denied, access to the internat.[198] The first visit by international monitors to the facility of which Human Rights Watch is aware is the CPT, in mid-April.[199] "Ilyas Makhmadov" believed that the guards stopped beating internat inmates because they had received information that representatives of a "human rights commission" were expected; it is possible that the commission referred to was the CPT.[200]

---

[196]Human Rights Watch interview with "Ilyas Makhmadov," Ingushetia, May 13, 2000..

[197]Human Rights Watch interview with Fatima Umarova, aged 40, Ingushetia, March 16, 2000.

[198]Daniel Williams, "U.N. Rights Chief Blocked From Chechen Sites; Russians Prevent Inspection Of Areas of Suspected Atrocities," *Washington Post*, April 3, 2000.

[199]CPT Press Release, "Second visit to the North Caucasus by the European Anti-Torture Committee," Strasbourg, May 2, 2000.

[200]Human Rights Watch interview with "Ilyas Makhmadov," Ingushetia, May 13, 2000.

Local Police Stations or Command Posts, and Abuse in Transit

Russian forces often use police stations as facilities for prolonged detention, since most are equipped with temporary holding cells. In some, crowded conditions over long periods rendered them inhumane, and detainees frequently reported that they were beaten and ill-treated while detained.

Many detainees who were arrested in January and early February 2000 were taken to the police station (also used as the local command post, or *komendatura*) in Znamenskoye before being transferred to Chernokozovo or released. Human Rights Watch interviewed nine people who had been detained and/or initially questioned there in mid-to late January.[201]

"Alimkhan Visaev" was arrested in late January in northern Chechnya, and was brought to Znamenskoye with thirty other men rounded up in his town. He spent four days at Znamenskoye, enduring beatings upon arrival and in his cell. He shared a police lock-up meant for two with seven other detainees:[202]

> [After we arrived at Znamenskoye] we were kept outside in the cold for two hours with our hands raised and the abuses began then. If you moved, you were beaten with rifle buts or kicked. I was beaten sporadically, beaten and kicked. We were beaten by about ten people, one was very tall, about two meters and heavy. I saw the face of one guard, who took off my Muslim hat—we were not allowed to look around at the others—he was tall, fat, over thirty years old and in camouflage uniform. I heard they were Volgograd OMON....
>
> We were kept outside for two hours and then ... we were called out one by one for interrogation.[203]

After being interrogated, "Visaev" was transferred to a temporary holding cell in a separate building:

> No threats were made in the police department, but after we were taken to [temporary holding cells] the beatings began.... There were eight

---

[201] Most provided little detail about the conditions of their detention in Znamenskoye, the bulk of the interview focusing on the subsequent abuses in Chernokozovo.

[202] To protect "Visaev's" identity, we do not disclose the name of the town where he was detained.

[203] Human Rights Watch interview with "Alimkhan Visaev," Ingushetia, March 22, 2000.

people in a cell for two, we put the beds together and four slept on the beds, four on the concrete floor.

Four people interviewed by Human Rights Watch, all of whom were arrested at their homes in Grozny on February 4, were held in Znamenskoye overnight before being transferred to Chernokozovo. During the journey, two of them reported, they were treated inhumanely, forced to lie on top of one another, which nearly suffocated those at the bottom of the pile. "Ali Baigiraev" was transferred on February 5 from Znamenskoye to Chernokozovo:

> [Thirty-two of us] were taken further on a bus [GAZ 53, prisoner-transport vehicle], loaded on top of each other like logs. The ones who were underneath were screaming, they were short of breath. If the ones on top moved, the soldiers hit him with a gun. When we arrived at Chernokozovo...two people underneath were unconscious. They just dragged them out.[204]

"Yakub Tasuev," who was transferred at the same time as "Ali Baigiraev," described the same incident to Human Rights Watch: "They loaded all thirty-two people into one small vehicle for transporting five or six people, it was a GAZ 53 for transporting the arrested. We were loaded on top of one another."[205] Although neither "Baigiraev" nor "Tasuev" reported how long the journey lasted, other interviewees transferred from Znamenskoye on other days said that the trip took approximately one hour.

Human Rights Watch has received isolated reports of other police stations or command posts where detainees are abused physically. "Rizvan Visangiriev," for example, was detained from March 3 to March 4 at the Staropromyslovski command post in Grozny, together with his son and twelve other men. He was beaten upon entry to the facility, gauntlet-style, also later on at night.

> That night they took us out one by one, put handcuffs on us, and beat us. The soldiers were all drunk. At about 11:00 p.m. or midnight, they took me out, covered my head with my jacket so I couldn't see anything. They threw me into a room with seven or eight people in it. I was taken out of the cell into the corridor and they put on handcuffs. In the room, three men beat me unconscious. They punched and kicked

---

[204] Human Rights Watch interview with "Ali Baigiraev," Ingushetia, February 21, 2000.
[205] Human Rights Watch interview with "Yakub Tasuev," Ingushetia, February 21, 2000.

me, beat me with batons and rifle buts. They said, "You killed our
people, you are a [rebel] fighter." It was dark and they were beating me
from all sides. I couldn't see who they were, I was trying to hide
[protect] my face. The beating lasted for about a half hour. They beat
me until I fell over, then held me up until I came round and beat me
again. This happened once or twice. I was still unconscious when they
took me back to the cell.[206]

"Visangiriev" and his son were released the following day after intervention by Chechens loyal to Bislan Gantimirov, a pro-Moscow Chechen leader. Prior to this, "Visangiriev" said, he had to sign a form stating that property confiscated from him had been returned and that he had no complaints against the police.

Some former detainees interviewed by Human Rights Watch were unable to identify the location where they were kept because they were blindfolded or otherwise kept in a state of complete disorientation. They were, however, clearly detained by Russian forces. One of them, "Zurab Aliev," was detained late at night on March 1 in his Grozny home by men he believes were FSB agents; they put a sack over his head and drove him to an undisclosed location within Grozny. He was kept alone in a pitch-dark cell, in what "Zurab Aliev" believes may have been the basement of an abandoned office building, although he could hear sounds such as coughing which made him think others were detained there as well. He was beaten and interrogated at the beginning of his detention, and then once every three or so days for the first two weeks, after which, he told Human Rights Watch, "they forgot about me." They would ask him about his activities and wanted him to collaborate with them by giving names of fighters he knew.

On one occasion, approximately one week after he was detained, "Aliev" was beaten while suspended by his feet, his head covered.

> I had the feeling they tied me with rope, they tied my feet together and pulled me up with some sort of pully. I had been standing on my feet, and they made a loop with the rope around my feet. They pulled the rope and I fell, then they wound it up, so that I was hanging. I don't really know how long I was in that position. They beat me, on my face,

---

[206]Human Rights Watch interview with "Rizvan Visangiriev" (not his real name), aged forty-seven, Ingushetia, March 29, 2000.

but mostly on my torso, in the area of my genitals and my lungs....
While hanging, they burned me with a cigarette, on my buttocks.[207]

"Zurab Aliev" was released on March 22, after being driven around for half an hour and thrown out of a car. When interviewed by Human Rights Watch, he was seeking medical treatment for injuries received as a result of the beatings, including kidney problems (including inflammation and a prolapsed kidney), prostatitis (inflammation of the prostate gland), and inflamed testicles.

---

[207]Human Rights Watch interview with "Zurab Aliev" (not his real name), aged thirty-three, Ingushetia, April 27, 2000.

THE BUSINESS OF RELEASE: EXTORTION, "AMNESTIES," AND THE THREAT OF RE-ARREST

Chechnya-related detainees are frequently extralegally "bought" out of detention. In fact, extortion of payment in return for releases occurs in so many cases, detention itself appears to have been motivated exclusively by the promise of financial gain, and release resembled a ransoming process. Others are released by amnesty, still others because authorities could find no evidence to justify further detention. Once released from custody, former detainees fear rearrest, in part because detaining authorities often fail to return identity or other important documents, even though one of the most common grounds for arrest is insufficient indentification documents.

Extortion

Of the thirty-five released former detainees interviewed by Human Rights Watch, twenty-one said that they or their relatives paid or were told to pay a sum for their release. The amount extorted usually ranged from 2,000 to 5,000 rubles,[208] depending on the seriousness of the charges against detainees. Relatives usually negotiate for the release of their loved ones through intermediaries, who often approach them and suggest possible "deals." In most cases, the intermediaries, primarily Chechens, work either at local police stations or for security agents, or have police or FSB connections. Many intermediaries prey on desperate families to extort large sums of money for the release of their relatives, and retain a portion of the payment for their services.

The Russian authorities' refusal to notify the families of those whom they detain, or to release lists of people in custody, facilitates predatory practices: in the vast information vacuum, lists of detainees are bought and sold. Human Rights Watch confirmed the role played by intermediaries by interviewing some of them and families who used them. One intermediary, who uses his former FSB contacts to approach prison authorities in Pyatigorsk, told Human Rights Watch that in late April, he had assisted in securing the release of three detainees; one had been "free," another cost 900 rubles,[209] and the third was released for U.S. $2,000.[210]

---

[208] Approximately U.S. $71 and U.S. $178, respectively.

[209] The sum of 900 rubles is about U.S. $32.

[210] Human Rights Watch interview, Ingushetia, April 23, 2000. He also claimed that he "bargained" with the authorities on behalf of a family over another man detained in the Georgievsk prison hospital in Pyatigorsk; although the asking price was initially U.S.

"Abu Uruskhanov" described in detail how one intermediary in Urus-Martan, a law-enforcement official, operated in collaboration with his superiors:

> There was a list on the street, posted outside [the internat]. Three or four guys would walk around nearby, and, for example, my relatives, they approached these guys. If my relatives found my surname, then they would approach one of these guys, saying we want to release him. Then the guy said 'Let's step aside and have a talk.' He told my brothers, 'I'll go upstairs and talk to my boss and I'll tell you the price.' When he came back he told them the price would be U.S. $600 plus a sub-machine gun. It is a very open process.[211]

"Uruskhanov" said that he believed he was beaten less severely because his relatives had opened negotiations about the payment. Four or five days after his release, on March 8 or 9, "Uruskhanov" returned to the internat to find that no lists had been posted, and that the intermediaries were selling information about who was inside to the crowd of relatives.[212]

"Marina Jambekova" borrowed money from friends and family to pay the $2000 demanded for her son. She paid this sum in early April, to an intermediary in the Chechen security services who had contacts with the Russians. Four weeks later, her son was "amnestied," Jambekova believed, because she paid the bribe.[213] In such cases, it is impossible to establish whether the bribe was actually paid over to Russian officials by the intermediary, or whether the detainee was released for other reasons.

Paying a bribe is no guarantee against repeated demands for money. A female relative of "Magomed Kantiev" told Human Rights Watch that the intermediaries whom she had paid for his release had come knocking at the door after he was amnestied on May 3; they were demanding more money and threatening that he could be rearrested if they refused to pay.[214]

"Alimkhan Visaev" was detained in mid-January with two brothers; they were released after eighteen days from Chernokozovo, after his relatives paid

---

$10,000 for the twenty-one year old man, he believes that the family probably paid $2,000 or $3,000 for their son.

[211] Human Rights Watch interview with "Abu Uruskhanov," April 26, 2000.
[212] Ibid.
[213] Human Rights Watch interview with "Marina Jambekova," Ingushetia, May 8, 2000.

[214] Human Rights Watch interview with "Magomed Kantiev," Ingushetia, May 13, 2000.

30,000 rubles. One of his brothers was rearrested, and again a ransom was demanded for him.

> My eldest brother [name omitted] was detained a second time... [He] was detained a week after our release, and taken to Znamenskoye, they asked for two guns in exchange. We paid about 10,000 rubles instead. Immediately following his detention, my brother's wife went to the person in charge of detentions in Znamenskoye. He told her to waste no time but to look for two guns.... When his wife said, "We are poor and have no money, where can I find money for two guns or dollars," the officer said that he knew [my brother] had five brothers that she should ask the brothers for money. After my brother's rearrest, I fled here.[215]

The sister of "Ali Baigiraev" described how she bought out her brother: a middleman from her village gathered money from three families for the release of three villagers. Ali Baigiraev had been detained on February 5 and spent one week at Chernokozovo.

> I learned from other people from the village whose relatives were also detained that you can buy out brothers and husbands from detention. I gave the money to the other villagers who were buying people out. Four or five people from the village gathered together, all of whom had someone detained, and gave money to one person in the village who had a detained relative, who was to deliver the money for those who were detained. People from the village told me how much to pay. I had to pay. The middleman from our village [said] how much each person costs. He said 2,000 rubles for each. At this time, we were trying to release three men. We paid 2,000 rubles for each. Thirty-two people were detained from my village, all have been released. All were bought out, for prices ranging from 2,000 to 5,000 rubles per person.[216]

Another case demonstrates how the dearth of reliable information about detainees' wherabouts facilitates predatory conduct by Russian authorities. Around March 22, a list of detainees who were held inside the Internat was read

---

[215]Human Rights Watch interview with "Alimkhan Visaev," Ingushetia, March 22, 2000.

[216]Human Rights Watch interview with "Ali Baigiraev's" sister, Ingushetia, March 25, 2000.

out by intermediaries to relatives maintaining a vigil there; the name of fifteen-year-old Adem Abubakarov was reportedly on the list. Intermediaries then told his mother, Khava Abubakarova, that Adem would be released on April 1 if the family paid $1,000. The family took a loan with 8 percent interest to pay this sum. When she attempted to pay the money, officials in the procuracy told her that Adem Abubakarov had been transferred to another facility, and showed her the internat's register with her son's signature.[217] The relatives could not locate him in any other detention facility, however. In late April or early May, Khava Abubakarova learned from officials that there was an order to "amnesty" her son as a juvenile, and that he was in either Stavropol or Pyatigorsk awaiting release.[218] When she went to Pyatigorsk however, intermediaries demanded a bribe of U.S. $3,000 for her son, although she had still received no official confirmation of his whereabouts.[219]

The authorities accepted bribes in exchange for civilians and rebel fighters alike. The head of administration of one Chechen village told Human Rights Watch that he had himself arranged with Russian authorities for the release of a captured fighter from his village in exchange for U.S. $5,000 and an automatic rifle.[220] "Ilyas Makhmadov," who was a fighter, was bought from detention twice, the first time for one sub-machine gun and the second time for another weapon and a sum of money unknown to him; his relatives also confirmed to Human Rights Watch that they had paid for his release. Describing the first detention, by Chechens loyal to Russian forces, he said, "It's a business for them, doing business with fighters and corpses. My uncle had to give them a gun, there was also money, but they said the release was some sort of amnesty, 'Gantemirov's amnesty.'"[221] Gantemirov is a leading pro-Moscow Chechen commander who often serves as an intermediary for families seeking the release of relatives.

---

[217]Human Rights Watch interview with Khamzat Abubakarov, Karabulak, Ingushetia, April 29, 2000.

[218]Human Rights Watch interview with Khamzat Abubakarov, Karabulak, Ingushetia, May 5, 2000.

[219]Human Rights Watch interview with Khamzat Abubakarov, Karabulak, Ingushetia, May 18, 2000.

[220]Human Rights Watch interview with head of administration of a Chechen town (name withheld), Ingushetia, April 27, 2000.

[221]Human Rights Watch interview with "Ilyas Makhmadov," Ingushetia, May 13, 2000. In 1999, the Russian government appointed Bislan Gantemirov, former mayor of Grozny, who was serving a prison term for embezzlement, as head of the pro-Russian forces in Chechnya. He was later removed.

A second witness reported that relatives managed to obtain the release of the brother of a high-ranking Chechen warlord, Arbi Barayev, from the internat facility in Urus-Martan:

> In the cell with me was Arbi Barayev's brother. They wanted a new Zhiguli [a Russian model car], twelve automatics and three pistols for him. He was released, [the relatives] paid what was demanded. But he was crippled, they damaged his spine. They tied his hands behind his back and they hung him by his hands and legs from the ceiling and beat him.[222]

In some cases, no intermediary is involved in the extortion process. On January 20, thirty-two-year-old "Issa Zagoyev"and a tractor driver were arrested by the Penza OMON while gathering wood in the forest outside Komsomolskoye. The main purpose for the detentions appears to have been extortion: the OMON soldiers did not turn Zagoyev over to investigative authorities; instead they immediately opened negotiations with Zagoyev's family about the price for his release, through the head of the local village council and a local pro-Moscow militia leader in Urus-Martan. At first, the soldiers demanded six automatic weapons in exchange for Zagoyev's release, but after several days of negotiations, they ultimately settled for 7,000 rubles, offered by his brother.[223]

Rearrest and the Threat of Rearrest

Released detainees live in well-founded, vivid fear of rearrest. Many men fear leaving their homes and are unable to seek refuge in neighboring Ingushetia; those who sustained serious injuries due to torture in custody so greatly fear rearrest that many do not dare leave their homes to seek treatment.

As Russian authorities do not return essential identity documents to detainees upon their release, and often they do not provide written acknowledgement that an individual had been detained, former detainees are vulnerable to rearrest during further identity checks. Without valid travel documents, former detainees remain virtual prisoners within their home communities. "Issa Habuliev" was severely tortured in Chernokozovo, but because he had no documents, feared travel even within Ingushetia to get needed medical treatment. His wife and her relatives traveled on multiple occasions to

---

[222]Human Rights Watch interview with "Issa Zagoyev," Ingushetia, April 8, 2000. A Zhiguli is a Russian-made compact car.
[223]Ibid.

Chechnya to try to obtain the documents, but were denied access to the prosecutor's office.[224]

Several people interviewed by Human Rights Watch had been detained twice, and had finally fled to Ingushetia in the hope of being free from further risk of rearrest. "Ali Baigiraev" was first arrested in January, after a sweep in his neighborhood, to be released after three days, badly beaten.[225] When he was rearrested on February 4 and taken to Chernokozovo, he queried the reason for his rearrest.

> I had been arrested earlier on January 11, and had been given a paper that they had nothing on me. When I was arrested this time, I saw the investigator who questioned me the last time and when I asked whether he remembered I had been checked before, the investigator confirmed it, but did nothing to get me released. They didn't care whether I really participated in the war, they were just carrying out their orders.[226]

"Idris Batukaev" was released from Mozdok on March 4, but was threatened with rearrest on the way home. He was again stopped at a checkpoint on his way to relatives in Ingushetia, where his documents were checked against the computer. "They checked a computer, asked for papers, and said that I had to be detained. We objected...I had just been released. They called the prison, where they confirmed that I had just been released."[227] He was then released, but warned to restrict his movements. "Idris Batukaev" was severely tortured during his detention at Mozdok but although his passport was returned, he has has not sought medical treatment in fear of being rearrested. In early May, his wife went to a friendly contact in the Russian administration, who confirmed that her husband's name was still "in the computer." "Idris Batukaev," in desperation, is considering obtaining false documents.[228]

---

[224]Human Rights Watch with "Issa Habuliev's" wife, Ingushetia, April 22, 2000.
[225]Human Rights Watch interview with "Ali Baigiraev's" cousin, March 25, 2000.
[226]Human Rights Watch interview with "Ali Baigiraev," Ingushetia, February 21, 2000.
[227]Human Rights Watch interview with "Idris Batukaev," Ingushetia, April 26, 2000.
[228]Human Rights Watch interview with "Idris Batukaev," Ingushetia, May 27, 2000.

OTHER VIOLATIONS OF THE RIGHTS OF INDIVIDUALS DEPRIVED OF THEIR LIBERTY

The systematic beatings, torture, and violations of international human rights and humanitarian law are only part of the abuses suffered by detainees in Chechnya. Detainees are held for extended periods of time in incommunicado detention, given no access to legal counsel, and are not informed of the status of proceedings against them.

The Russian government has not declared a state of emergency and has given no notice of derogation from its obligations under the European Convention for the Protection of Human Rights and Fundamental Freedoms or under the International Covenant on Civil and Political Rights. Without any extraordinary legislation, the regular provisions of the Russian criminal code and code of criminal procedure are applicable, as are international human rights standards.[229]

Prolonged Incommunicado Detention and "Disappearances"

He's nowhere. Not among the living, not among the dead
A woman about her missing nephew.

If I knew he was dead, I would cry three days, mourn, and be able to move on, but this way, I don't know, I know he's alive, but don't know where he is.
A father about his missing fifteen-year-old son.

Russian authorities withhold information about whom they have in custody, and do not allow detainees to communicate with their families or others, even those held for many months. After large-scale arrests began in February 2000, Human Rights Watch researchers in Ingushetia were constantly contacted by anxious individuals desperate for assistance in learning the fate of their relatives

---

[229] Experts from the Council of Europe concurred with the Secretary General of the Council of Europe's opinion that, even though Russian authorities attempted to argue that there was a de facto state of emergency in Chechnya, the fact that it had not been formally declared and that derogations had not been made in law meant that the provisions of the European Convention on Human Rights continued to apply in full. Council of Europe document, "Addendum to the Consolidated report containing an analysis of the correspondance between the Secretary General of the Council of Europe and the Russian Federation under Article 52 of the European Convention on Human Rights," SG/Inf(2000)24 Addendum, June 26, 2000.

whom Russian authorities had detained. Informal lists of detainees rumored to be in different facilities circulate but are not a source of reliable information.[230] Relatives sometimes learned the whereabouts of their loved ones by paying bribes. Many maintain a steady vigil outside the detention centers where they believe their relatives may be detained.[231]

Relatives travel to detention facilities throughout Chechnya and parts of southern Russia seeking information in vain. Zina and Roza Iznaurova searched for their thirty-four-year-old brother, Yakub Iznaurov, at eight different facilites in Chechnya and other parts of southern Russia. According to the Iznaurovas, OMON detained Yakub Iznaurov on February 5, 2000, during a passport check, claiming they would return him shortly.[232] The Iznaurovas watched as OMON loaded their brother—together with neighbors Islam Asuev (age twenty-six), Magomed Gabangaev (age forty-nine), and Said-Emin Jamaldaev (age twenty-nine)—into a prisoner transport vehicle, pulled knit caps over their eyes, and tied their hands with wire.

Yakub Iznaurov's sisters and other relatives searched for him throughout Chechnya, including at detention centers in Chernokozovo, Tolstoy Yurt, Chervlyonnaya, Gudermes, Znamenskoye, Grozny, and outside Chechnya in Mozdok, Pyatigorsk, Vladikavkaz, and Nalchik. Guards at Khankala would not allow them near the premises to ask authorities about him. The authorities at all of these facilites refused to give the Iznaurov family information about Yakub Iznaurov's whereabouts, or of the other three men detained with him.

On some occasions, prison officials conceal that they are holding particular individuals. For example, on January 16, 2000, Chernokozovo officials denied to Marina Jambekova that they were holding her son "Abdul Jambekov." Jambekov confirmed to Human Rights Watch, after his release, that, in fact, he was in Chernokozovo at that time. "Marina Jambekova" subsequently

---

[230]By mid-April, 2000, Human Rights Watch received nineteen such lists, many of which contained duplicate information, containing a total of 130 names. Interviewees could not identify the source of the lists, but suggested they were compiled by released detainees and sympathetic prison staff.

[231]A journalist who was in Urus-Martan saw a group of a dozen relatives waiting there when she visited Urus-Martan in late March. Human Rights Watch interview with Natalie Nougayrede, of *Le Monde*, by telephone, May 31, 2000.

[232]Iznaurov is originally from the Okruzhnaya district but has a residence permit for Kalmykia. Human Rights Watch interview with Zina and Roza Iznaurova, Ingushetia, April 20, 2000.

approached authorities in and around Tolstoy Yurt, Znamenskoye, and Naur, who were rude and refused to give her any information.

"Marina Jambekova" subsequently went to Chernokozovo every day for eight days. Together with several other women also searching for their relatives, she wrote a joint appeal to the prosecutor asking for a brief meeting, which went unanswered. "Marina Jambekova" eventually found out that her son was in Chernokozovo, and was able to give guards food packages for him, for which she received receipts with his signature.[233]

"Marina Jambekova" again lost track of her son on February 18, when he was transferred; Chernokozovo authorities refused to disclose his destination. On Feburary 21, she tried to try to find her son at the Pyatigorsk pre-trial facility. Authorities there denied he was there, when indeed he was.[234] She remained unaware of his whereabouts until March 15, when she received a letter from her son, who at that time was pre-trial detention in Stavropol (he was transferred there on February 22). "Marina Jambekova" eventually paid U.S. $2,000 to secure the release of her son, and charges against him were dropped when he was "amnestied" on May 3, 2000.

Denial of access to legal counsel

Russian authorities routinely and in almost all cases deny detainees in Chechnya access to counsel. Furthermore, they often fail to inform detainees of any charges against them, and forbid detainees from reading the charges against them.[235] Massive intimidation in custody and lack of even a pretense of due process rendered virtually impossible the ability to challenge the legality of custody or seek redress for due process violations.

Russian law and and international standards uphold the individual's right to competent legal assistance from the moment of detention and during interrogation.[236] Access to counsel in this context is an important safeguard to

---

[233] Human Rights Watch interview with "Abdul Jambekov," Ingushetia, May 7, 2000.

[234] Human Rights Watch interview with "Marina Jambekova," Ingushetia, March 28, 2000, and with "Abdul Jambekov," May 7, 2000.

[235] Article 9(2) of the ICCPR obliges states to inform detainees of the charges against them.

[236] Under article 48(2) of the Russian constitution, criminal suspects have the right to counsel from the moment of detention, and under article 58 of the criminal procedure code police are obligated to inform them of this right. Principle 17(1) of the Body of Principles for the Protection of All Persons under Any Form of Detention or Imprisonment (Body of

prevent torture, ill-treatment, and other means of coercing confessions, all of which affect detainees in Chechnya. Effective legal counsel can also be important so that a suspect can be advised on how and whether to challenge the basis for detention.

The Parliamentary Assembly of the Council of Europe, following its rapporteur's visit to Chernokozovo on March 11, objected to detainees' lack of access to legal counsel.[237] Special Representative Kalamanov responded with skepticism to the allegation, but made a "personal commitment" to ensure that detainees would obtain it.[238] Legal representation continued to be a priority for Special Representative Kalamanov as late as July 2000, and as of this writing Council of Europe experts and Special Representative Kalamanov were still trying to organize legal representation for detainees.[239]

Of the thirty-five former detainees interviewed, only one said that he was ever offered the advice of a lawyer while in custody. The vast majority scoffed when Human Rights Watch asked if they had requested a lawyer. "Idris Batukaev," who was detained in Mozdok for more than three months, gave a typical response: "How dare I [ask for a lawyer], when at the same time they put a gun to my head or threatened to cut my ears off. I didn't dare ask."[240] "Abu Uruskhanov," who was held at the Urus-Martan internat laughed, "There were no lawyers there."[241]

"Movsar Larsanov," the one detainee who was offered access to counsel, rejected it, skeptical that the legal assistance would be genuine. When he was interrogated at Chernokozovo on January 29, "[the investigator] said I could have a lawyer. I said I didn't need one. It would be useless [when at other times] they said, 'who are you, you are nothing.'"[242]

Principles), which applies to all people who are detained, states that "a detained person shall be entitled to have the assistance of a legal counsel. He shall be informed of his right by the competent authority promptly after arrest and shall be provided with reasonable facilities for exercising it."

[237] "Chechnya rights official pledges inmate lawyer inquiry," Agence France-Presse, March 12, 2000.

[238] "Russia: Chernokozovo inmates to get lawyers after PACE visit," Itar-Tass News Agency/BBC Worldwide Monitoring, March 11, 2000.

[239] Council of Europe press release, "Council of Europe mission continues to make significant progress in Chechnya," Strasbourg, July 21, 2000.

[240] Human Rights Watch interview with "Idris Batukaev," April 26, 2000.

[241] Human Rights Watch interview with "Abu Uruskhanov," April 26, 2000.

[242] Human Rights Watch interview with "Movsar Larsanov," May 25, 2000.

Most interviewees shared "Movsar Larsanov's" skepticism about seeking access to counsel. In one egregious case, when "Magomed Kantiev" was taken for interrogation there were two men present, a major and a colonel, who told "Kantiev" that he was being charged with article 208(2) of the Russian criminal code, which deals with the organization of and participation in illegal armed formations. "There was a guy who said I could sign the papers or not, it made no difference. I signed the *sanktsia* (detention orders) on detention for two months." The "major and colonel" did not give "Kantiev" a copy of the document with the charges against him. When asked if he was provided a lawyer, "Kantiev" laughed, and said, "Where would I get a lawyer? Even if you wanted one there aren't any. I didn't ask for one, they said themselves it was useless to ask for a lawyer."

Law enforcement officials also routinely failed to inform detainees about the nature and cause of the charges against them. In those cases when detainees were informed they had been charged, law enforcement officials would not allow them to read, let alone have a copy, of the charges. "Movsar Larsanov," for example, told Human Rights Watch:

> The procurator said the case was under investigation, that I had been charged, as though I were a fighter, with article 208, but they couldn't prove it. From the beginning they told me that I had been charged. They gave me the warrant and I signed the paper. But they didn't give me a copy of the charges or the warrant, they didn't even give me enough time to read what I was signing.[243]

"Abdul Jambekov" had a similar experience. He was beaten during interrogation to coerce him into signing a report.[244] He signed the report which was in his own words, but the guards started to beat him when he refused to sign the warrant: "They wanted me to sign a piece of paper. I asked if it was possible to read, even to look at the papers that I was supposed to sign but they didn't let me. They said I should just sign it."[245]

---

[243] Human Rights Watch interview with "Movsar Larsanov," Ingushetia, May 25, 2000.

[244] "Abdul Jambekov" used the Russian word for a police report *protokol,* but it was unclear whether he was refering to an arrest report or interrogation report.

[245] Human Rights Watch interview with "Abdul Jambekov," Ingushetia, May 7, 2000.

Most, however, were simply never informed about the status of the charges (if any) against them. "Aslanbek Digaev" was detained from January 23 to May 3 after being taken from his house ostensibly to check his identity. He told Human Rights Watch: "I always asked them to explain to me who I was, was I convicted, was I charged, was I detained, what stage the proceedings were. The only explanation I got was that 'you are a bandit-terrorist. To be Chechen, that's your crime.'"[246]

---

[246] Human Rights Watch interview with "Aslanbek Digaev," Ingushetia, May 16, 2000.

RECOMMENDATIONS

To the Government of the Russian Federation
Human Rights Watch documented the endemic nature of torture in the criminal justice system in Russia in a 1999 report, *Confessions at any Cost: Police Torture in Russia*, (New York: November, 1999). The report makes detailed recommendations to the Russian authorities on approaches to end the practice of torture in police custody and prisons. Human Rights Watch again calls on the Russian government to implement those recommendations as a matter of priority.

End the Practice of Torture
- Direct all Russian Federation forces—including Ministry of Defense troops, OMON, and other Ministry of Interior troops as well as all staff working at detention centers—to cease violations of international human rights and humanitarian law, including torture, beatings, physical abuse, rape, and other forms of cruel and inhuman treatment at detention facilities and during the arrest process; instruct those forces that perpetrators of such violations will bear criminal responsibility; and investigate all allegations of torture, and initiate appropriate disciplinary and criminal measures;

- Inform all detainees immediately of the grounds of arrest and any charges against them. Provide all detainees with immediate and regular access to attorneys, and allow detainees to petition for review of their detention without delay. Accord procedural rights to all persons detained and/or accused of crimes; inform the families of detained persons of their detention, the reason for and location of the detention. Allow families of detained persons regular contact with detainees;

- Review all confessions to ensure that they were not extracted under torture, drop all pending charges based on confessions extracted under torture, and refrain from bringing charges based on confessions extracted under torture. Enforce the inadmissibility of statements extracted by force in all legal proceedings, other than those brought for redress of abuse; and

- Direct all Russian Federation forces to immediately end the current practice of extortion, which forces relatives of detained persons to pay money to Russian officials to obtain their release. Conduct a full investigation into the widespread practices of extortion, and prosecute all officials found to have engaged or tolerated extortion in conditioning the release of detainees.

Ensure accountability for torture, and compensation and rehabilitation for victims
- Investigate fully allegations of abuse and improper treatment of those in detention, fully prosecute all officials found to have used or tolerated the use of excessive force; and grant compensation to victims;

- Investigate the deaths of detainees at the Chernokozovo detention facility, the Internat facility at Urus-Martan, and the Khankala military base, in accordance with the standards set forth in the United Nations Principles on the Effective Prevention and Investigation of Extra-Legal, Arbitrary and Summary Executions. The government must prosecute to the fullest extent of the law all officials found to have used or tolerated the use of excessive force; and grant compensation to relatives of the victims;

- Make publicly available all reports from investigations conducted into human rights violations in Chechnya, in particular the investigation into torture and ill-treatment in Chernokozovo required by the Council of Europe's Committee for the Prevention of Torture and Inhuman or Degrading Treatment or Punishment (CPT); the outcome of which was due by June 2000;

- Make publicly available regularly updated figures on the number of individuals charged and arrested for security-related crimes in Chechnya, with information on the nature of their alleged crimes and the places of their detention. Registers of the names and places of detention should be readily available; and

- Provide resources for the physical and psychological rehabilitation of torture victims, supporting nongovernmental initiatives. Recognize the extreme cultural stigma attached to acts of sexual violence in Chechen culture and support programs for rehabilitation which will not make those who seek rehabilitation vulnerable to further societal consequences.

Ensure access by the international community
- Provide unrestricted access to detainees and detention facilities by representatives of the International Committee of the Red Cross (ICRC), as well as the Assistance Group of the Organization for Security and Cooperation in Europe (OSCE) and representatives of the U.N. High Commissioner for Human Rights;

- Facilitate prompt visits by the U.N. Working Group on Arbitrary Detention; the U.N. Special Rapporteur on Violence Against Women; the U.N. Special Rapporteur on Extrajudicial, Summary or Arbitrary Executions; the U.N. Special Rapporteur on Torture; the Special Representative of the Secretary-General for Children and Armed Conflict, and the Special Representative of the Secretary-General for Internally Displaced Persons;

- Cease delaying the deployment of the Assistance Group of the OSCE to Ingushetia and Chechnya; and

- Agree to the immediate deployment in Ingushetia and Chechnya of an independent, international commission of inquiry with a mandate to investigate violations of international humanitarian law by both sides in the conflict, and the ability to recommend prosecutions in appropriate cases.

To the Special Representative for Human Rights in Chechnya Vladimir Kalamanov

- Investigate allegations of torture, abuse in detention, arbitrary arrest, extortion, and summary executions in detention facilities. Attempt to establish the identity of the parties responsible for abuses, and recommend their prosecution where appropriate. Ensure that adequate mechanisms are instituted to protect the safety of victims and witnesses;

- Monitor all places of detention, particularly in temporary holding facilities operated by the Ministry of Interior and Ministry of Defense, in and around Chechnya for compliance with international standards. Ensure that detainees have the opportunity to be interviewed in private and in confidence about their treatment;

- Through regular field visits, ensure that victims have access to the staff of the Special Representative throughout Chechnya as well as in settlements of displaced people outside the Republic. In particular, ensure that persons who have had their identity documents confiscated and thus cannot travel have access to the staff of the Special Representative;

- Visit areas of recent "mop-up" operations to ensure that the conduct of Russian troops is in accordance with international standards;

- Publish regular, public reports on the findings and activities of the Special Representative, as well as on the actions taken by the relevant authorities in response to those findings; and

- Seek from the Russian government its report on violations in Chernokozovo from December 1999 to February 2000, as requested by the CPT, and recommend to President Putin that the report be made public.

To the International Community
Representatives of various international organizations and governments, including the United Nations, the European Union, and the United States have repeatedly exhorted the Russian government to investigate abuses committed in Chechnya and to hold those responsible accountable. Although the Russian government had not undertaken a credible investigation, on April 25, 2000, the United Nations Commission on Human Rights failed to call for the creation of an international inquiry into the abuses, instead calling once again on the Russian government to conduct an investigation. The Russian government continues to make no meaningful progress on accountability for abuses in Chechnya. Accordingly, Human Rights Watch once again calls on representatives of the international community to:

- Establish an international commission of inquiry to observe, investigate, and report upon human rights and humanitarian aspects of the military operation in Chechnya, and that have the ability to recommend prosecutions in appropriate cases. The commission would also provide assistance to Russian authorities in the carrying out of investigations; and

- Communicate with Chechen, Russian and international nongovernmental organizations involved in the treatment of, and advocacy for, torture victims in Russia, and support the U.N. Voluntary Fund for Victims of Torture.

In addition, the OSCE, the U.N., and the Council of Europe have mechanims and institutions authorized and competent to deploy on-site either short-term missions, in the case of the U.N. thematic mechanisms, or a longer-term presence, in the case of the OSCE. Human Rights Watch believes that fuller transparancy in exposing abuses would be better achieved with an active presence on the part of these institutions, each acting in its own capacity.

Recommendations

United Nations

On April 25, 2000, the United Nations Commission on Human Rights adopted a resolution expressing its concern about allegations of abuse in Chechnya, "notably in the alleged 'camps of filtration,'" and requesting the relevant rapporteurs and working groups of the commission to undertake missions to the region, and urged the Russian government to facilitate such missions. At the time of writing, none of those mechanisms had received permission of the Russian government to visit the region.

- The High Commissioner for Human Rights, Mary Robinson, should continue her commitment to working on Chechnya. A deadline should be set for her return visit to the region, to which the Russian government has committed itself. The visit, which should be carried out as soon as possible, should include visits to some of the detention centers documented in this report where abuses are believed to be continuing to date;

- The High Commissioner for Human Rights should continue to engage the Russian government on its implementation of the April 25 resolution; and

- The U.N. Special Rapporteur on Torture, the U.N. Special Rapporteur on Extrajudicial, Summary or Arbitrary Executions, the Special Representative of the Secretary-General for Children and Armed Conflict, and the U.N. Special Rapporteur on Violence Against Women should vigorously pursue the visits mandated by the April 25 resolution and investigate allegations of abuses relevant to their mandate. The U.N. Working Group on Arbitrary Detention should also join this initiative.

To the Council of Europe

The Council of Europe's engagement in Chechnya peaked in April, when out of concern for Russia's lack of respect for human rights the organization's Parliamentary Assembly suspended Russia's voting rights and requested the Committee of Ministers review Russia's continued membership. The Council of Ministers did not do so, however, and the organization's stance subsequently became much less critical. It justified this by citing "improvements" in the situation, and describing the much-delayed deployment of international Council of Europe expert staff to the office of Special Representative Vladimir Kalamanov as indicative of Russia's good faith to address human rights violations. Council of Europe member states refer to this office, and its collaboration with Council of Europe staff, as a substitute for other mechanisms that might lead to accountability for abuse, in particular, an inter-state complaint.

Similarly, UNHRC member states pointed to this arrangement as substituting the need for an international commission of inquiry. For this reason, Human Rights Watch believes the work of this office should be closely scrutinzed and completely transparent.

Generally, the Council of Europe has not employed all the tools available to it to ensure that Russia adheres to the human rights standards membership in the organization requires. In particular the relevant bodies and/or member states of the Council of Europe should:

- File interstate complaints against the Russian Federation at the European Court of Human Rights, as recommended by the Parliamentary Assembly of the Council of Europe, to hold Russia to account for violations, including torture, committed in detention centers in and around Chechnya, as well as other incidents of gross violations of international humanitarian law such as the civilian killings in Alkhan-Yurt and the Staropromyslovski and Aldi districts of Grozny;

- Ensure that Russia complies fully with the mandatory "thorough and independent" investigation into allegations of ill-treatment from December 1999 to mid-February 2000 in Chernokozovo that was requested by the Council of Europe's Committee for the Prevention of Torture and Inhuman or Degrading Treatment or Punishment (CPT) in March 2000, whereby Russia was required to "inform the CPT of its outcome within three months." The Council of Europe should continue to encourage Russia to make public the reports of the CPT to the Russian government and the Russian government to the CPT on detention conditions in the North Caucasus, including its report into the abuses at Chernokozovo;

- Insist on the independence of Council of Europe staff provided to the office of the Presidential Representative on Human Rights in Chechnya, including their freedom of movement and their right of unfettered communication with the Council of Europe Secretariat. Ensure that their role within the office, as anticipated by Secretary-General of the Council of Europe Walter Schimmer immediately preceding their deployment, continues to be "an important step to restore the human rights situation in the region back to normalcy and bring those responsible for human rights violations to justice;" and

Recommendations 95

- As envisioned by its 1994 Declaration, the Committee of Ministers of the Council of Europe should set in motion a special investigation into Russia's compliance with its Council of Europe commitments. It should take into account the reports of the Secretary-General and experts which concluded that Russia has already failed to live up to its obligations to respond to the Secretary General under the Article 52 procedure.

To the Organization for Security and Cooperation in Europe
On April 11, 1995, the OSCE established the Assistance Group to Chechnya. Its mandate, explicitly reaffirmed by all OSCE member states, including Russia, at the November 1999 Istanbul Summit, provides that it will, among other things, "promote respect for human rights and fundamental freedoms," and "facilitate the delivery to the region by international and nongovernmental organizations of humanitarian aid for victims of the crisis, wherever they may be located." The Assistance Group enjoys "all possible freedom of movement on the territory of the Chechen Republic and also on the territory of neighboring subjects of the Russian Federation, if so required for the performance of its tasks." The OSCE Assistance Group left the region when hostilities broke out in September 1999; as of this writing, the Russian government has actively impeded the group's redeployment.

- As is foreseen under the existing Assistance Group mandate, the OSCE should immediately deploy an expanded Assistance Group delegation to Chechnya and Ingushetia: to gather evidence of violations of human rights and humanitarian law committed in Chechnya; to report publicly on any such abuses and make recommendations to the Russian government to curb abuses and hold those responsible accountable; and to monitor the treatment of displaced persons and advise the Russian authorities and international agencies with respect to needed humanitarian assistance;

- In accordance with the 1994 Code of Conduct on Politico-Military Aspects of Security, articles 30 and 31, the OSCE must insist on Russia's obligations to investigate abuses committed by Russian Federation troops in Chechnya and prosecute those found responsible. The OSCE should insist that Russia keeps the Chair-in-Office and the OSCE Permanent Council informed on progress in this regard; and

- The OSCE Assistance Group should cooperate with any investigation undertaken by the Russian government, but any monitoring or other activities by the Assistance Group should remain independent and distinct from the activities of Russian government institutions.

To the International Monetary Fund, the World Bank, the European Bank for Reconstruction and Development and Bilateral Donors

- Immediately suspend payment of all pending loan installments payable to the Russian Federation for unrestricted general budgetary spending, including pending World Bank payments under its structural adjustment loans. Signal that such payments will not resume until the Russian Federation takes meaningful steps to limit the civilian toll imposed by its military operation in Chechnya. Such steps should include serious, transparent, and impartial investigations of abuses committed and accountability for those responsible, and acceptance of a sustained international monitoring presence in Chechnya and Ingushetia and full cooperation with its activities; and

- Refuse to negotiate any new loans or to renegotiate any existing loans until the above steps are taken.

To the European Union and the United States

Discussing alleged abuses in Chechnya before the United Nations Commission on Human Rights, Portuguese Foreign Minister, Jaime Gama, speaking on behalf of the European Union, stated that a "serious and independent investigation must be carried out without delay in order that those responsible can be brought to account." Addressing the same forum, U.S. Secretary of State Albright called for "prompt and transparent investigation of all credible charges." To date, the Russian government has failed to undertake a serious investigation of abuses in Chechnya. It is therefore necessary for the E.U. and the U.S. to press forward for a two-track process of accountability involving both national and international inquiries. Specifically, the E.U. and the U.S. should:

- In bilateral and multinational public and private communications with the Russian government, emphasize that abuses committed by Russian government forces in Chechnya, such as torture, summary executions, rape, pillage, and the deliberate destruction of civilian property, amount to war crimes and serious violations of international law;

- Continue to press the Russian Federation to undertake a thorough, transparent investigation of abuses committed in Chechnya and to hold accountable those responsible, warning that accountability is a

Recommendations

nonnegotiable minimum condition for enhanced political, economic, and security relationships with the Russian Federation; and

- Oppose payment of any pending loan installments payable to the Russian Federation for unrestricted general budgetary spending, including pending World Bank payments under its structural adjustment loans. Assert the position that such payments should not resume until the Russian Federation takes meaningful steps to limit the civilian toll imposed by its military operation in Chechnya and hold those responsible for abuses accountable. Such steps should include serious, transparent, and impartial investigations of abuses committed and accountability for those responsible, acceptance of an international monitoring presence in Ingushetia and Chechnya and full cooperation with its activities, and meaningful steps to curb looting and the destruction of civilian property in Chechnya.

APPENDIX 1: KNOWN PLACES OF DETENTION IN CHECHNYA

In most cases, detainees did not know the legal status of the institution where they were detained. Information on the official function and the authorities responsible for the following confirmed places of detention in most of the cases below comes from the Council of Europe's Committee for the Prevention of Torture and Inhuman or Degrading Treatment or Punishment (CPT).

Pre-trial detention Facilities (Sledstvennyi izoliator or SIZO), under the authority of the Ministry of Justice:

- Grozny (SIZO)*
- Chernokozovo (SIZO)*+
- Vladikavkaz (North Ossetia) (SIZO)*+
- Pyatigorsk (Stavropol territory) (likely *Belyi Lebed*, SIZO)*+
- Stavropol (SIZO) (Stavropol territory)
- Territory Hospital at Colony No. 3, Georgievsk (Stavropol Territory)+

Temporary detention facilities (Izoliator vremennogo soderzhaniia or IVS), under the authority of the Ministry of Internal Affairs:
- Chervlyonnaya Station (according to Russian authorities, this facility was closed in April, 2000)*
- Naurskiy District Department of Internal Affairs*
- Shali District Department of Internal Affairs*
- Temporary Internal Affairs Department of Grozny Selsky District (Tolstoy Yurt)*
- Oktyabrskyi District Temporary Department of Internal Affairs, Grozny+
- Zavodskyi District Temporary Department of Internal Affairs, Grozny+
- Temporary Department of Internal Affairs, Gudermes+
- Khankala Military Base of the Allied Group of Armed Forces (FSB and MVD operate temporary holding facilities in Khankala)+
- Temporary Department of Internal Affairs, Shelkovskaya+
- Urus-Martan; (there are three temporary holding facilities in Urus-Martan: FSB, and the district and regional MVD; at least one of them is in the Internat boarding school)+
- Mozdok District Department of Internal Affairs (North Ossetia)*

Appendix 1: Known Places of Detention in Chechnya

Places of Detention whose status is unknown to Human Rights Watch:

- Former holding facility, Goryacheistochnenskoye (Tolstoy Yurt) (according to inteviewees, this facility was closed in mid-February, 2000; it was empty when visited by the CPT on its first visit at the end of February)*
- Solyonaia Balka military base (Grozny) (at least during January, 2000)
- Znamenskoye police station (at least during January and February, 2000)
- Ersenoi military base (at least during April and May, 2000)
- Achkhoi Martan police station

* visited by the CPT on its March 4 to 26 February, 2000 trip to the North Caucasus.
+visited by the CPT on its April 20 to 27, 2000 trip to the North Caucasus.